Trustee Responsibility for Academic Affairs

Trustee Responsibility for Academic Affairs

Richard P. Chait, Project Director
Kenneth P. Mortimer
Barbara E. Taylor
Miriam M. Wood

Table of Contents

Foreword

Academic affairs are by definition the central concern of an educational institution. Academic affairs have to do with teaching and learning, with courses of instruction, with the organization of departments, divisions within colleges and universities, with intellectual standards and requirements, with the quality and deployment of the faculty, with the quality of supporting services and facilities, with the allocation of resources to support all these efforts, in short, with all that makes a college or university an *academic* institution.

What is the role of trustees with respect to this central academic core? What responsibilities, if any, have they for the educational programs, personnel policies, and resource decisions? How can they carry out their responsibilities for reviewing and approving institutional policies and strategies?

The founding members of college and university boards knew what they wanted. They set the course, marshaled the resources, and zealously safeguarded the purposes and missions of the institutions they helped to establish. As time went on, however, first administrators and then faculty gradually assumed control of what should be taught and who should do the teaching. This was natural enough. Administrators and faculty were, and are, the professionals, qualified by training, experience and commitment to establish, modify and fine tune the complex academic process.

Consequently, for the last hundred years administrators and faculty have been left very largely in charge of internal academic matters, while trustees have concentrated on external questions such as buildings and grounds, fund raising, and public and governmental relations. As volunteer lay men and women who are not professional educators, they were warned, quite properly, not to meddle in courses of instruction. They assumed, or were encouraged to assume, less properly, that they should stay away from educational programs entirely.

That this division of functions works as well as it usually does is a triumph of forbearance and goodwill over logic. It does not always work well.

Presidents and faculties sometimes have assumed a posture inconsistent with board-approved goals, creating conflict, disorganization, and loss of effectiveness. Boards of trustees have sometimes interfered in purely internal academic issues with disastrous results. Shared cultural and educational goals, an expanding economy and educational system, and the widely held though incorrect belief that trustees were not legally responsible for the internal operations of their institutions helped to conceal inconsistencies and to promote ambiguities.

The heart of the problem lies in the fact that responsibility for internal affairs and external affairs cannot be completely separated. The physical plant, for example, presumably exists to serve the educational needs of the institution. Decisions about classroom buildings, laboratories, libraries, and other elements of the plant should be related to and, in fact, depend upon decisions in the academic area. Again, while the budget is determined in part by nonacademic factors such as rate of endowment income, volume of current gifts, and interest on indebtedness, its basic purpose is to support the educational program. Therefore, the always painful tradeoffs on budget decisions need to be ever tempered by genuine understanding of short-term academic problems and long-term academic goals.

Today the favorable factors that long alleviated the board/academic affairs problem have given way to stringent conditions that make it more acute. The student demographic decline and diminishing resources have brought an era of faculty retrenchment and hard choices about new versus existing programs. Formerly accepted academic goals and standards are being challenged in a many-sided struggle for survival and the maintenance or restoration of excellence. Is a certain new venture imaginative and promising, or is it merely a desperate attempt to bring in revenue even at a cost in quality or integrity of purpose?

Trustees are responsible for maintaining the integrity of the institution's goals, for making certain that the educational programs are consistent with the mission, and for approving budgets which reflect the best educational thinking. This does not mean that trustees should engage in curriculum planning and revision or that they should get involved in the decisions to promote Instructor X or terminate Instructor Y. Such particulars should be left to the academic professionals. Trustees should receive recommendations from the president, or from the faculty through the president.

The trustee role is to ask questions: Are we clear about our mission? Is this new program consistent with that mission? What are the financial consequences of approving this or that change? Without getting involved in faculty appointments and promotions, in individual promotion and tenure decisions they should demand that clear academic policies be adopted and consistently followed.

On the academic stage, the president plays the lead role. He or she is the indispensable intermediary between the faculty and the board. His job or hers is to translate often conflicting faculty viewpoints and recommendations into concrete proposals that will advance the purposes of the institution. The board has the right, indeed the obligation, to ask of the president: What is your vision for this institution over the next ten years, and how do you propose to achieve it? Trustees should look to the president for educational leadership, and provide to the president the support that effective leadership requires.

The authors of this volume recommend that academic affairs are too important to be left *entirely* to educators. Trustees hold the institution in trust. They are the guardians of its mission. They must keep in mind future generations and their needs as well as the needs of those now on campus. They must understand the educational values which the academic program seeks to realize.

No standing board committee serves a more significant role in helping the governing board fulfill its reason for being than the Academic Affairs Committee.

John W. Nason
Keene, N.Y.
July 1984

Introduction

The origins of this volume lie in a perception widely shared among college and university trustees and presidents that the Academic Affairs, or Educational Policy, Committee is one of the most vital yet, too often, least effective board committees. Considerable uncertainty and ambiguity exist about lay participation in such a sensitive, professional domain. Faculty and administrators remind trustees now and then that academic affairs constitutes the heart of the institution and that trustees should not attempt to function as specialists.

To help trustees constructively discharge their responsibilities for overseeing the academic realm without interfering with the president or usurping the prerogatives of the faculty, the Association of Governing Boards commissioned a study of "The Role of the Trustee in Academic Program and Personnel Planning." The basic assumption of the project was that a board enlightened and informed about academic affairs should prove to be beneficial to the president, the chief academic officer, and the faculty leaders.

Academic programs should reflect an institution's mission and principal purposes. Their fulfillment in turn depends largely on the caliber of the faculty and academic administration, and on the prudent allocation of resources. Over the long run, an institution's ability to survive and flourish hinges on its academic success.

Although a board may have no more crucial realm of responsibility, academic affairs has not always enjoyed the attention of trustees. Some board members are more familiar and thus more comfortable with finance, development, and physical plant, and some faculty members and administrators prefer that trustees extend only "benign neglect" to academic affairs. As a result, administrative and financial issues tend to dominate board deliberations while the academic matters are overlooked, to the detriment of institutional vitality.

Realization that academic affairs constitutes the core of an institution can tempt boards to err in the opposite direction. Excessive involvement can be as harmful as neglect, since academic affairs is an area in which faculty members and academic administrators have the primary concern, possess the professional expertise, and normally operate under substantial delegations of authority.

Trustees and committee members must recognize the need to strike a balance between too much and too little. Too much involvement by trustees can be construed as overstepping their policy-making role—substituting their judgment for that of faculty and administrators appointed to conduct the institution's academic affairs. Too little participation, on the other hand, can be construed as an evasion of responsibility in the one area that deals with the essence of the institution. The sensitivity of the board's position, then, is obvious.

The key question for a board of trustees is not whether to participate in academic affairs but how to participate usefully. We believe this book will contribute significantly to a board's efforts to answer that question.

The study, directed by Richard P. Chait, former Associate

Provost of The Pennsylvania State University, had four principal components.

1. A series of essays by members of the study group that constitute Chapters I through V of this volume.

2. A national survey of 600 college and university trustees and presidents on trustee involvement in academic affairs. Highlights of the survey are presented in Appendix B. The complete survey results are available in *Trustee Responsibility for Academic Affairs: Results of a National Survey* by Barbara E. Taylor, available from AGB.

3. Eight in-depth case studies that examine different approaches to trustee participation in academic affairs. These cases, summarized in Appendix C and available from AGB, may be particularly useful for a board retreat or workshop.

4. A Self-Study Survey (Appendix A) designed to assist an Academic Affairs Committee to develop or refine an appropriate role and to facilitate a self-assessment of the committee's performance. While addressed to members of an Academic Affairs Committee, the survey should also be helpful to boards with other arrangements for overseeing educational policies and programs.

Chapter Synopses

Chapter I, by Richard Chait, describes the responsibilities of an Academic Affairs Committee within the context of the unique academic culture. To ensure that educational policies are consistent with mission and strategy, Chait encourages trustees to seek information relating policy proposals to organizational objectives.

In Chapter II, Miriam Wood offers 11 guidelines related largely to process. The first three delineate a perspective for the Academic Affairs Committee that recognizes the professional nature, distinct culture, and tradition of shared governance of colleges and universities. The next four address the issue of channels of communication between the Academic Affairs Committee and the various campus constituencies, emphasizing the value of structured, formal arrangements. Guidelines 8-10 stress the need for information on *strategic* policy matters. The final guideline discusses periodic self-study and recommends other potential sources of feedback. The chapter closes with a description of three dominant operating styles of Academic Affairs Committees.

In Chapter III, Richard Chait treats of academic personnel policies and urges trustees to concentrate on policy objectives. A discussion of the trustees' role in tenure policy includes questions trustees might pose about the criteria, the review process, tenure decisions, and the operation and effectiveness of a tenure system. Chapter III also considers the general principles of retrenchment, as well as policies and procedures that need to be established with substantial faculty and administrative participation. The second half of the chapter focuses on incentive and reward structures and faculty evaluation. For example, the Academic Affairs Committee should not be a party to individual salary decisions or performance appraisals, but should participate in the determination of policy objectives for a compensation plan and an evaluation scheme. The chapter suggests questions trustees can ask and data trustees can request to ensure that compensation plans are congruent with stated objectives and that the evaluation process is consonant with the announced purposes. The chapter concludes with a discussion of faculty development.

In Chapter IV, Kenneth Mortimer considers academic program approval, review, and closure, and the locus of authority for each. When new programs are proposed, Mortimer recommends that the Academic Affairs Committee ask questions that relate the proposal to mission, strategy, cost, need, and the quality of available faculty and facilities. For the review of existing programs, the attention of trustees should be directed to the purposes of program review, and the process, the criteria, and the actions that may result. Mortimer offers five important caveats about the economics and politics of program closure, then considers the need for a board to reserve the right to close programs, to require a well-planned phaseout, and to defend the decision to constituencies.

In the final chapter, Barbara E. Taylor demystifies the

academic budget, which she says should be an expression of institutional priorities. After reviewing the organizational features that complicate academic budgeting, Taylor describes the strengths and weaknesses of three approaches: the free market approach, rational budgeting, and incremental budgeting. She then guides the reader through the budget with explanations of revenue and expenditure categories, cost concepts, and productivity measures, and suggests questions for trustees to ask. She cites the phases and participants of budget making, and concludes by discussing financial ratios as a technique to gauge institutional financial condition.

* * * * *

I wish to acknowledge the role of AGB's Executive Vice President Tom Ingram, whose perseverance and commitment resulted in a foundation proposal and a successful project, and the role of Richard P. Chait, who ably directed this study. Kenneth Mortimer, Barbara E. Taylor, and Miriam Wood served as key members of the project team and chapter authors, and offered a splendid combination of ability, energy, goodwill, and wit. Day by day the project operated smoothly due largely to Linda Henderson at AGB and Glenna Younginger at The Pennsylvania State University.

And, finally, we owe a special debt of gratitude to the Exxon Education Foundation and the Ford Foundation for their generous support, and to the many trustees and presidents who participated in our survey and case studies and who offered us advice and guidance along the way.

Robert L. Gale
President
Association of Governing Boards
of Universities and Colleges

The Authors

D**r. Richard P. Chait** is former Associate Provost at The Pennsylvania State University and director of the AGB study of the Role of Trustees in Academic Affairs. He is a trustee of Maryville College (Tennessee) and an associate of the Cheswick Center in Boston. He has served as a consultant to the W. K. Kellogg Foundation, the Lilly Endowment, the National Institute of Education, the Council on Foundations, the American Council on Education, and numerous colleges and universities. Prior to joining Pennsylvania State in 1980, Dr. Chait held positions at the Institute for Educational Management at Harvard, and as Assistant to the President of Stockton State College. He is a coauthor of the book *Beyond Traditional Tenure*, published by Jossey-Bass in 1982.

Dr. Kenneth P. Mortimer is Executive Assistant to the President for University Affairs, and Professor of Higher Education and Public Administration at The Pennsylvania State University. He is currently chairing the National Institute of Education's Study

Group on the Condition of Excellence in American Higher Education. He has also served as director of the Center for the Study of Higher Education at Pennsylvania State and as Special Assistant to the Senior Vice President for Administration and Consultant to the Provost. His most recent research, the *Project on Reallocation,* encompasses more than 300 interviews with college and university chief academic officers on reallocating people, programs, and budgets within the area of academic affairs. Dr. Mortimer served as the project director for AGB's study on improving trustee selection and has been a consultant on matters of academic management and governance to a variety of institutions, associations, and private foundations.

Dr. Barbara E. Taylor is Director of the Institute for Trustee Leadership at the Association of Governing Boards. She has been Assistant to the Vice Chancellor for Academic Programs, Policy and Planning at the State University of New York and has served as a staff member in the Office of the Provost at The Pennsylvania State University. In addition she was a primary investigator for the Association of Governing Boards study of the role of Trustees in Academic Affairs, and recently coauthored an AGB publication on *The Academic Affairs Committee.* Dr. Taylor writes and consults on college and university trusteeship, planning, and finance.

Dr. Miriam M. Wood is an independent consultant who works with various non-profit agencies. Her principal activity is research in higher education administration, including the role and practices of college and university governing boards. Her major study of trusteeship, *The Board of Trustees and the Small Private College,* is to be published by The Johns Hopkins University Press in 1985. Dr. Wood has served as a trustee of a liberal arts college and as a member of the board of directors of a child care agency, a library, and a private foundation. Her articles on trusteeship have appeared in *Educational Record* and *The Harvard Business Review.*

The Role and Responsibilities of the Academic Affairs Committee

RICHARD P. CHAIT

The study group on the trustee role in academic affairs recommends that a board of trustees establish an Academic Affairs or Educational Policy Committee expressly charged to oversee academic affairs. This area is simply too vital to be subsumed under another committee or, worse, left outside the scope of committee assignments.

The study group believes that a college or university will be served better over time by a structure that ensures (or at least makes more probable) that some trustees will be particularly knowledgeable about and sensitive to academic affairs. Some boards have both faculty affairs and educational policy committees with the former responsible for personnel matters and the latter for academic programs. Because these areas are so interrelated, a single committee is recommended. Other boards, typically with nine or fewer members, operate as a Committee of the Whole. The advice and suggestions offered here can be applied to these boards as well.

The complex and demanding task of the Academic Affairs Committee is to ensure that academic personnel, programs, and budgets are properly integrated in support of the institution's mission. In executing this task, the committee should: (1) require that the administration develop institutional strategies and policy objectives; (2) ask incisive questions about goals, policies, and strategies; and (3) accept, reject, or recommend changes in the wide sweep—and not the details—of these proposals.

The committee's scope should encompass four areas discussed at length in the chapters noted parenthetically. It should:

• ensure that faculty personnel policies and procedures complement academic priorities. (Chapter III)

• ensure that the educational program is consistent with both institutional mission and strategies. (Chapter IV)

• ensure that the academic budget reflects the institution's academic priorities. (Chapter V)

• ensure that the institution assesses the effectiveness of its academic activities. (Chapters II through V)

In discharging these responsibilities, the Academic Affairs Committee must strike a sensible balance. It must understand the difference between seeing that appropriate actions are taken and taking those actions itself. The committee should be tenacious yet restrained, self-directed yet receptive to the contributions of others. By asking questions, committee members must help the administration and faculty to confront academic challenges squarely. Such "activity through inquiry" by the committee will help ensure that the institution's results are consistent with its aims. This requires a prior step: the development of institutional goals.

A Mission Statement

The foremost purposes of a college or university are usually expressed in a mission or goals statement that sets broad institutional objectives and articulates central institutional values. A mission statement answers such questions as: What "business" are we in? What needs and markets do we serve? What services and products do we offer? How, or through what means, are these services and products offered? Trustee responsibility for academic affairs begins here.

In *The Future of Trusteeship* (1975), John Nason cited ten major responsibilities of trustees; four were categorized as "standard expectations" and six as "new demands" for the years ahead. Among the "new demands" Nason listed first "clarification of purposes."

> The clarification of purpose or purposes is a job for faculty, administration, and *trustees* . . . . The articulation of purpose in specific and operational terms is not likely to be made unless governing boards demand it and are prepared to take an active part in formulating the statement . . . . It is the board's responsibility to see to it that there is a clear statement in writing to which every trustee can honestly subscribe and that every faculty member will recognize as setting the direction of the institution. (pp. 18-19)

Discharging this responsibility is not easy. The ambiguous nature of colleges and universities impedes development of a crisp and distinctive mission statement. Many colleges and universities are not quite sure what their primary areas of endeavor and major markets are. Consequently, many mission statements are long on rhetoric about excellence, quality, and the discovery and transmission of knowledge, but short on the specific means and strategies to achieve these results. As competition intensifies for scarce resources and students, such bland statements of purpose will no longer suffice. Today strategic plans must be developed to attain the goals articulated in mission statements.

The Strategic Plan

The mission statement describes a destination. The strategic plan provides the road map to get there. It leads the college or university from where it is today to where it wants to be tomorrow.

In *Academic Strategy* (1983, pp. 143-153) George Keller describes six characteristics of a strategic plan. Paraphrased, these six elements are:

1. A college or university and its leaders are active rather than passive about their position in history. Strategic planning entails a belief that you can to some extent shape your own destiny as well as be shaped by external forces.

2. The college or university looks outward and is focused on keeping the institution in step with the changing environment. Institutions rely not on self-assertion but on a biological model of continuing adaptation to their powerful, changing social environments.

3. Academic strategy is competitive, recognizing that higher education is subject to economic market conditions and to increasingly strong competition.

4. Strategic planning concentrates on decisions, not on documented plans, analyses, forecasts, and goals. It is action-oriented. It constantly asks: What shall we do? How shall we decide? Where do we put our attention and energy? It is people acting decisively and in concert to carry out a strategy that they have helped devise.

5. Strategy-making marries rationality and artfulness, financial facts and politics. It is participatory and tolerant of controversy. Participation is imperative. There need not be a full consensus, but most of the key people need to be in reasonably close agreement.

6. Strategic planning concentrates above everything else on the fate of the institution.

In a word, strategic planning requires that an institution first establish an overall direction and then attempt to match internal strengths to external opportunities. Without a strategic plan, most colleges and universities will be hard pressed to succeed and some will be hard pressed to survive.

Strategy should be formulated by senior administrators with faculty consultation, but the overall plans should be reviewed and ultimately approved by the board. When confronted with policy recommendations or critical decisions, the board must tirelessly ask: Are these new recommendations consonant with our strategic plan?

Policy Making

Translating mission statements and strategic plans into action occurs through policy formulation and operational decisions about academic personnel, programs, and budgets.

The process must start with information. With guidance from the president and the chief academic officer, the Academic Affairs Committee should establish an "information calendar" that specifies what data the committee needs to receive, in what form, and how often. Only a fraction of the flow of the *management* information system might be needed to serve *governance* responsibilities. The committee might wish to see, for example, annual staffing plans, profiles of student characteristics, or data on resource shifts and program quality. In the chapters that follow we suggest a number of other data elements that the committee probably will need.

The information base will also help a board committee to coalesce. Shared information fosters a sense of community and collegiality. An information calendar should reduce, if not eliminate, requests for information by individual trustees, requests that are often perceived as interference in administrative affairs. The information calendar can act as a neutral intermediary between the committee and other constituencies while establishing the spheres and even the standards of committee responsibility.

With adequate information at hand, the Academic Affairs Committee will be ready to consider matters of policy. In most cases, a recommendation on academic policy will reach the committee after consideration, often protracted, by the faculty and the administration. The committee's role will be to ask questions about the proposal and assess the responses. The general questions that follow suggest the tone the committee inquiry may take:

What are the policy objectives? A statement of policy objectives should precede a statement of policy. The proponents of a particular policy change should be able to articulate their aims. A change in compensation plans, for example, might be designed to reward merit, to motivate performance, to ensure equity, to reduce expenses, to respond to competition, or to meet some combination of these objectives. From the perspective of the committee, the critical question must always remain: *What are the main purposes the policy is intended to serve?*

As a corollary, the committee might also ask: *What evaluations will be undertaken to determine whether our purposes are realized?* Some measures of effectiveness should accompany any new policy initiative. Questions by the committee should encourage the administration to incorporate data on the policy's outcomes into future reports.

Is the proposal aimed at a new objective, or is it merely a new approach to an established objective? If the policy objective is not new, committee members might want to pose some questions about the apparent ineffectiveness of current policy.

Has there been compliance with existing policies and procedures in this area? Recruitment of women and minorities, for instance, may lag because departments or schools have not followed regulations. Or perhaps the policies are unclear, unknown, or unavailable. The institution can remedy these problems through clarification or dissemination of policy. Perhaps different incentives or sanctions are needed. New policies, per se, are not likely to resolve issues of compliance.

Are there any conflicts among policy objectives or between policies and procedures? One policy objective might be to achieve high quality; another might be to achieve low costs. One goal might be to reduce tenure levels; another might be to add women and minorities to the permanent faculty. Conflicts in purpose rather than inadequacy of policies might be the problem to resolve. Or policies and procedures might work at cross purposes. A university might have such cumbersome review procedures for reallocation that it cannot respond promptly to an urgent opportunity.

Does the weakness lie with the policy or with its administration? The Academic Affairs Committee should avoid recommending changes in policy when the real problem may lie elsewhere. The converse also applies: People should not be changed when policies may be faulty. Sometimes both people and policies need to be changed. Some personnel problems are problems of policy execution, not of policy. On the other hand, many problems associated with affirmative action, for example, derive from ambiguous, contradictory, or weak policies.

If the administration, after consultation with the faculty, and the Academic Affairs Committee agree that a policy change is called for, the committee should request that the administration:

- state or restate the policy objectives;
- enumerate the policy alternatives congruent with the objectives;
- present a persuasive argument for the alternative recommended;
- review the nature and extent of the consultation process and report the sentiment of the faculty; and
- present a draft policy for discussion.

If the committee senses that it is policy administration that has faltered, it needs to adopt a different course of action. Where the performance of certain administrators appears to be at issue, the committee might invite the president to explore possibilities that range from professional development to reassignment. If the situation or context presents a deeper problem, then the committee might ask the administration to consider strategies, such as reallocation of resources or restructuring of the organization, that alter the circumstances and improve the environment. As with most policy actions, any of these will entail trade-offs.

The line of inquiry presented here presumes that the Academic Affairs Committee and, indeed, the Board of Trustees will be reviewers, not initiators, of academic personnel policies. On infrequent occasions, the committee or the board might perceive a need unrecognized by the faculty or the administration, or the trustees might conclude that the campus community will not, without some stimulus, inaugurate a policy discussion. In these cases, the trustees' role should be to encourage consideration of the issue and delegate development of policy drafts. The committee should not itself write policy, although it might enunciate broad principles that a new policy should honor.

The Academic Culture

Missions, strategies, and policies are formulated within the context of a specific organizational culture. As Stonich (1982, p. xviii) remarked: "All organizations have cultures that delineate in an unoffical and usually unspoken way, the 'rules of the game.' It is how things are really done. Recognizing the ramifications of the firm's culture is especially critical when implementing strategy because, in many respects, culture—more than any other element—dictates what can and will be done." Guideline 1 of Chapter II suggests some ways in which trustees can assess a campus' culture. Here we note some of the characteristics that distinguish colleges and universities from other organizations, particularly corporations. Four are particularly important. (Chait, 1979, pp. 36-40)

1. Colleges and universities typically function with goals that are ambiguous, diverse, and difficult to measure, whereas the goals of a business are usually quite precise, quantifiable, and readily understood.

2. Academic institutions tend to diffuse power. Many managerial decisions are made at the department, school, or college level. In the spirit of collegiality, or shared governance, most significant institutional decisions are made in conjunction with faculty. Indeed, based on the precedent established by the U.S. Supreme Court in *National Labor Relations Board v. Yeshiva University* (1980), the NLRB has determined that faculty at several independent colleges are more akin to managers than employees and thus not eligible to bargain collectively. Trustees wary of collegiality might be reassured somewhat by observing the currency now attached in the corporate sector to participatory, or Japanese, management style.

3. Many faculty members are attracted to their profession by the prospect of considerable work autonomy and little direct

supervision, especially after tenure. Self-direction and the freedom to determine course content and research agendas are hallmarks of the academic professions, especially at preeminent colleges and universities. Deans and department heads, for sound reasons, strive to establish collegial rather than supervisory relationships with faculty members.

4. Colleges and universities only marginally employ economic reward structures, in part due to the scarcity of discretionary money, but also because of the difficulties of performance appraisal, and the relative attractiveness of other rewards such as freedom, intellectual fulfillment, prestige, and recognition.

Trustees should be sensitive to these idiosyncrasies which shape and define the culture of a college or university and also imply certain behavioral norms. Administrators do not, as a rule, issue orders or demand conformity. Faculty do not readily tolerate abrogation of the collegial process or preemptions of faculty prerogative. The bedrock values of most campus communities virtually demand that trustees participate but not dictate.

Committee Membership

The success of an Academic Affairs Committee rests at least as much on the quality of the committee members as on the quality of the advice the committee receives. Unfortunately, on some campuses the committee has not commanded the prestige warranted by its responsibilities, and talented and effective trustees are often assigned to other committees, notably budget and finance.

The board and the president need to ensure that some of the ablest trustees serve on the Academic Affairs Committee. It should not be difficult to make such service attractive in light of the degree to which the intrinsic values of the college or university are expressed in academic affairs issues.

Members of the Academic Affairs Committee should have a consuming interest in the institution's academic mission and objectives. New committee members should be prepared to devote sufficient time to absorbing needed background information. They should be comfortable with collegial traditions and open communication among the committee, the administration and the faculty.

To coordinate activities and plans within the board, the Academic Affairs Committee might profitably include a member of the Budget Committee. In addition it might be wise if the committee's chairperson, ideally a trustee with experience in educational matters, also serves on the Executive Committee. To facilitate communication and to enrich the committee's perspective, the board might choose to appoint faculty and student members to the committee (see Guideline 4 of Chapter II).

CHAPTER II

Guidelines for an Academic Affairs Committee

MIRIAM M. WOOD

With advice from other members of the study group, the author developed 11 guidelines to assist trustees in their analysis of academic matters. These guidelines define the Academic Affairs Committee's perspective on academic issues, its relations to the administration and faculty, and its role in setting educational policy.

The Committee's Perspective on Academic Affairs

Guideline 1: Trustees should become familiar with the mission, academic programs, and distinctive organizational culture of their institution.

Colleges and universities differ in a variety of respects from the corporations, law firms, government agencies, churches and small businesses in which many trustees pursue their vocations. No organizational difference is more conspicuous than the tradition of shared governance on most campuses whereby faculty participate in the control of educational policy. On a practical level, the results of shared governance vary, and trustees at different institutions will observe diverse patterns.

Sometimes the professional authority of a faculty is virtually inviolate, but collegial in expression, so that educational policy is formulated through consensus between faculty and administrators. At other institutions, educational policy emerges through negotiation and political compromise among powerful groups within the faculty which tend to resist administrative leadership. On still other campuses the president and academic vice president are able to exercise substantial influence in guiding or directing the faculty.

Whatever the local circumstances, members of the Academic Affairs Committee will find that there are many distinctive rules, formal and informal, which influence the academic administration, and the committee should ensure that these customs are taken into account in the board room. In this role, the committee functions not as a defender of the faculty or a curriculum expert, but as an interpreter of processes and issues which might be more familiar to committee members than to others on the board.

An important first step in acquainting trustees with the institution's mission is an orientation which provides a well organized overview of faculty affairs and educational programs. When the president and chief academic officer fail to take the initiative, the committee chairperson should request that such an introductory program be scheduled.

Each year, members of the Academic Affairs Committee should be provided with informative materials, such as brochures from the admissions office(s), faculty handbooks, and college catalogs. For more substantive insights into the quality and intellectual character of the institution, committee members should turn to the institution's most recent regional accrediting report and the self-study which preceded it. At universities, committees might also wish to review specialized accrediting reports issued for individual schools or academic programs, as well as any other evaluations conducted by outside panels. A précis of all of these reports should be provided and should be read by every trustee; for members of the Academic Affairs Committee, perusal of the original documents is recommended.

Regularly scheduled educational presentations by deans, faculty members, or students provide another opportunity for trustees to keep informed about academic programs and organizational culture. Members of the Academic Affairs Committee should suggest to the chief academic officer topics for such presentations congenial to trustee interests.

Guideline 2: Thoughtful, common sense questions and observations about broad academic issues are never out of place in the Academic Affairs Committee.

Once acquainted with faculty governance and the content and organization of the curriculum, members of the Academic Affairs Committee are in a position to provide a unique "insider-outsider" perspective on education policy. Because faculty members and administrators might lack objectivity when their own professional interests and programs are at stake, general questions and thoughtful observations by lay people encourage, or even force, the participants to reevaluate basic premises and policy implications.

Given the deliberative nature of shared governance, change can take months or years; however, members of the Academic Affairs Committee must guard against inadvertently becoming captive to the status quo. Through questions and comments, committee members should encourage the president and chief academic officer to engage in the kind of broad, reflective thinking that may be crowded out in the hurly-burly of daily pressures.

Some trustees hesitate to ask questions about academic matters because they feel uninformed or fear appearing naive, yet certain essential and legitimate questions require no expertise. For example, it is appropriate to ask, and often revealing to learn, who was consulted in arriving at a recommendation and which alternative proposals were considered. Occasionally trustees become concerned about offending an administrator who seems to resent questioning. Ticklish as these circumstances can be, it is the right and duty of committee members to persist with legitimate questions. (Conversely, the committee should not indulge any member whose inquiries are clearly irrelevant or an intrusion into administrative matters.)

> *Guideline 3:* The Academic Affairs Committee should recognize the prerogatives of a professional faculty in the development of educational policy but must not relinquish the prerogatives of the board as the ultimately responsible body.

In the subtle interplay of substance and process in academic policymaking, the governing board is in a position to balance the narrower concerns of a campus, school, or department against the overall scope and quality of the educational program. In practice, therefore, the Academic Affairs Committee's singular contribution rests on its ability—and willingness—to isolate and resolve academic issues that no other group on campus has the objectivity and authority to address.

For example, if the president and chief academic officer have not prepared a retrenchment plan for fear of an adverse effect on morale, the Academic Affairs Committee can, in executive session, serve as a forum to discuss whether the development of a contingency plan outweighs the negative consequences of the planning process; or the trustees can take pressure off the president by making public the committee's insistence on realistic planning. The committee must remain equally vigilant and future-oriented when the institution is doing well, and must expect that in times of prosperity, attempts to contain expansion will be unpopular.

Whether times are good or bad, it is often not easy for an Academic Affairs Committee to identify the truly important issues which can be overshadowed, or even obscured, by routine activities preoccupying the faculty, the chief academic officer, and thus the committee. Nor is it easy to be an advocate of an institution and at the same time maintain the critical distance that gives trustees their special perspective. Yet some degree of detachment is essential if the committee is to provide the governing board with wise and resolute guidance concerning the academic issues that are most vital to the institution's welfare.

Channels of Communication

Since the Academic Affairs Committee receives and reviews information and, when appropriate, recommends action to the full board, the question of how and from whom the committee obtains its information is of special importance. Trustees and regents are sometimes puzzled to find information from the administration contradicted in part by informal communications they receive from faculty members, students, parents, or legislators.

Although institutions differ in the sources of information officially made available to members of the Academic Affairs Committee, precedent or the board's bylaws normally designate the president, the chief academic officer, and perhaps the administrative secretary to the board as official contacts. Other "official" sources of information might include professors and students who attend meetings of the committee as invited guests, as elected representatives of the faculty senate or student government, or on some other basis.

Guideline 4: Trustees should work with the president and chief academic officer to develop appropriate procedures for consulting faculty and students.

Some Academic Affairs Committees, primarily in the private sector, now have faculty representation which provides trustees with firsthand exposure to the faculty point of view. Since faculties, like other professional groups, exhibit a diversity of opinion, trustees should clarify whether the one or two faculty members meeting with the committee are expressing personal views or conveying a synthesis of faculty opinion. At institutions where faculty representatives are appointed by the president there is sometimes the sense, real or imagined, that the faculty member is chosen because he or she is unusually sympathetic to the administration. Appointment or election of the representative through the faculty governing structure eliminates this ambiguity.

The opinions of faculty representatives might, quite properly, influence the decisions of the Academic Affairs Committee, but trustees should take pains that this avenue of communication does not undercut the authority of the president and academic vice president. Committee members must also be mindful that the advice of faculty representatives, whether they participate as voting members or as invited guests, is a supplement to, not a substitute for, the formal actions of the faculty governing structure. To this end, the ongoing activities of the faculty senate should be reported regularly to the committee by the chief academic officer or another designated official.

Sometimes a professor or an administrator from another institution might be asked to join the board and serve on the Academic Affairs Committee as a means to bring an informed perspective and added credibility to the committee both on campus and in the board room. However, an undue deference to the views of this one member may place an unfair burden on him or her and cause an unintended evasion of responsibility by other members of the committee.

The possible role of students on the Academic Affairs Committee is ambiguous, and only a minority of committees have student members. Some trustees and administrators feel that students can claim no legitimate role in academic decisions. Other trustees prefer to form an opinion on certain matters only after developing a sense of "what the students think." Most trustees genuinely enjoy contacts with students and recognize that a multiplicity of viewpoints is the rule rather than the exception for most student bodies. The student government typically appoints or elects representatives to serve on the Academic Affairs Committee.

Guideline 5: Trustee members of the Academic Affairs Committee should meet regularly in executive session.

If faculty and students participate in the Academic Affairs Committee, and if sunshine laws permit, it is wise to reserve some time at the beginning or end of each meeting for the trustees to meet in executive session. This procedure provides an orderly and socially comfortable arrangement for the departure of faculty and students when the committee wishes to discuss sensitive issues or to test for consensus.

The regularity of the executive session is important. If the executive session is an unusual event, it becomes a red flag to the faculty and student representatives and others on campus; rumors might circulate. The role of the president and chief academic officer in the executive session must be treated with the greatest delicacy, and at most institutions these two officers will regularly participate. If in some unusual circumstance their participation is not desired, the committee chair should not ask them to leave until the faculty and student participants have had time to depart. This protocol will protect the authority and dignity of senior administrators.

Guideline 6: Recommendations regarding faculty and curriculum are normally presented to the Academic Affairs Committee by the president or chief academic officer; rejection of a recommendation requires diplomacy.

It is common practice among colleges and universities for the chief academic officer to bring policy issues to the committee and often to prepare the agenda for the meeting, usually subject to the approval of the committee chair. This practice does not imply that the committee is a rubber stamp, but it acknowledges the roles of the faculty, dean, and president and enables trustees, in the limited time available to them, to focus on the strategic implications of various issues.

A committee that rejects administrative recommendations will find that its opposition erodes the authority of the president and chief academic officer. However, if differences of opinion do occur, the committee should discuss with the president and chief academic officer how this action will appear to on-campus constituencies, especially the faculty. Perhaps the item can be withdrawn for further consideration. If not, the committee should try to couch its vote or recommendation to the board in a context which will minimize any loss of credibility by the administration. The committee should also consider how detailed a public explanation to offer. Often confusion about the committee's rationale can be minimized if one individual—perhaps the committee chair—serves as a spokesperson to whom all inquiries can be referred.

To avoid the complications of a negative vote by the committee, experienced presidents and chief academic officers often present items "for information" well in advance of a formal decision and involve trustees, where possible, in intermediate deliberations. "Never surprise the board" is the watchword of administrators who wish to avoid public differences with trustees. Where early notice and prior consultation are not part of the administration's style, members of the Academic Affairs Committee might wish to suggest this approach.

Guideline 7: Opportunities to build bridges between the Academic Affairs Committee and the faculty should be arranged by the president or chief academic officer.

Many presidents arrange occasions for faculty and members of the Academic Affairs Committee, as well as other trustees, to meet together in informal settings. These can include receptions or dinners for trustees and faculty members or special visitations where faculty are asked to make informative presentations to board members. Trustees and regents find such occasions both instructive and enjoyable. For members of the Academic Affairs Commitee these are particularly valuable opportunities to season their judgment and insight about curriculum issues and academic politics.

Occasionally campus politics prompts presidents to discourage trustees or regents from conversing casually on campus with faculty members or students. They worry that a trustee who gets an earful of a maverick viewpoint might come to the next Academic Affairs Committee meeting with an unrealistic or disruptive agenda. Trustees themselves occasionally speak wryly of being "collared" by a faculty member or student with an axe to grind. However, a courteous hearing is the appropriate response and is usually all that is expected. (See Guideline 10.)

The board may also undertake more formal bridge-building activities. For example, a joint task force of faculty and trustees might be established to consider an issue such as the future of the liberal arts curriculum, the consequences of technological change, or the educational needs of the corporate work force. Or it might be appropriate for the Academic Affairs Committee to meet occasionally with the parallel committee of the faculty senate.

Quality, Scope, and Accuracy of Information

Guideline 8: The Academic Affairs Committee should confine itself to policy, planning, and strategic issues.

A number of subtle influences tend to narrow the focus and limit the time horizon of the Academic Affairs Committee, and the committee must continually resist these. Most notably, administrators immersed in the daily activities of an institution may inadvertently bring to the committee issues of narrower rather than broader scope. To forestall this tendency, the committee should foster broad-gauged thinking by requiring administrators to present an annual memorandum on academic strategy.

Such a memorandum should not be confused with the long-range academic plan which is usually based on compromises already made or goals already achieved. A memorandum on academic strategy raises questions, highlights problems, and suggests future directions which may not have been formally approved by the faculty. Prepared annually for the Academic Affairs Committee by the president or chief academic officer, the memorandum describes from a strategic perspective the directions in which the academic leadership wishes to guide the faculty and the institution.

In requesting the memorandum, the Academic Affairs Committee should establish with the president a time horizon within which projections of pertinent data can reasonably be made. Many organizational strategists consider three to five years a realistic time horizon, while a ten year horizon may involve too many assumptions to permit safe predictions and sound proposals.

The content of the memorandum should answer the question: What is your vision for this institution and how do you expect to achieve it? This approach gives the president an opportunity to talk about his or her vision for the institution in the context of realistic assumptions about enrollment levels, student interests, faculty talent, financial resources, and environmental constraints. Most important, discussion of academic strategy encourages the senior administrators and the trustee committee to work cooperatively on issues of policy and strategy that will shape the institution's future course.

Guideline 9: The Academic Affairs Committee should urge the administration to gather and analyze data on the external environment.

As discussed in Chapter I, the development of a strategic plan requires coming to terms with the external environment. Certainly it is essential that the president and chief academic officer evaluate the potential impact upon the institution of events and trends beyond the campus gates, and often committee members are well-situated to identify and prompt consideration of important environmental issues.

Data and projections useful for strategic planning and policy analysis are available from outside sources such as state and federal government and higher education interest groups. However, trustees should not be expected to scrutinize the data. The role of the trustee is to encourage academic officers to take into account such outside factors before preparing plans and recommendations and then to listen carefully to the resulting analysis.

Indeed, to provide a receptive and perceptive audience for

the educational plans and visions of the president and chief academic administrator is a rarely acknowledged but very important responsibility of the Academic Affairs Committee.

> *Guideline 10:* Problems and questions that come to the Academic Affairs Committee through the "grapevine" should be referred to the chief academic officer or the president.

Many trustees find that their understanding of campus events is broadened through newspaper stories, trustee-faculty friendships, and chance encounters on and off the campus. Often these sources of information can add dimensions to documents and discussions trustees are exposed to in the course of official meetings. Less constructively, the informal network functions as a conduit for gossip and personal interests. Whatever the circumstances, each trustee must recognize that perceptions of "the facts" and "the truth" are no more uniform in colleges and universities than in other organizations, and ultimately each committee member must judge the accuracy of the information received or the perspectives offered. Occasionally the disparity between official and unofficial communications becomes great enough to provoke concern, and in that case a trustee should turn to the academic officers to resolve the discrepancy.

> *Guideline 11:* The Academic Affairs Committee should perodically undertake a self-study of the committee's role, responsibilities, and operating style.

From time to time the members of the Academic Affairs Committee might feel uncertain about the scope of their responsibilities, the appropriateness of the issues they address, and the role they play. More generally, members of the committee may be concerned about the adequacy and effectiveness of the committee's efforts. These are all sound reasons for the committee to undertake a self-study periodically, perhaps every three to four years.

The study group on the trustee role in academic affairs developed a self-assessment survey (see Appendix A) for the

Academic Affairs Committee designed to help members review academic issues and evaluate the appropriateness of their role in light of the distinctive character of the institution they serve.

The committee should not overlook other sources of feedback. The views of the board chairperson, the president, and the chief academic officer can be solicited informally by the chair of the committee. Committee members should create an environment in which student and faculty representatives to the committee feel free to offer comments or suggestions. Where the committee feels inadequately equipped to deal with a certain issue, the members can ask for stronger direction and more guidance from the administration. In addition, some boards, with the support of the president, may find it useful to seek assistance from the AGB Board-Mentor Program or from a consultant.

The effectiveness of a committee's work and the nature of the committee's relationship with various constituencies is influenced by its operating style as well as by the substance of its decisions. Boards exhibit many different styles, even among different committees of the same board. In this author's observation, the members of an Academic Affairs Committee tend to follow one of three styles:

• *The populist.* These are the committee members who are eager to know "what the faculty thinks," to make themselves accessible to students, and to exchange views with the campus community. Sometimes they overstep proper bounds without realizing that excessive zeal in soliciting opinions may be interpreted as showing a lack of confidence in the administration.

• *The consultant.* This type of committee member is less interested in collecting faculty views than in developing his or her own recommendations and thus trying to influence academic affairs from the top down. Occasionally these trustees use their expertise in, for example, law or business to perform substantive services for the college. The danger comes when volunteer assistance shades over into unwarranted interference.

• *The privy councillor.* Trustees in this mode operate as a sounding board and loyal adviser to the president. Privy councillors react rather than initiate and deliberately limit their exposure to faculty and students. Such committee members use probing questions and pointed comments to influence the thinking of the president and chief academic officer.

Any of the three styles can be effective; likewise, any can be harmful if committee members are unable to adjust to changing circumstances. Thus, the more effective committee members, whatever their customary style, are flexible enough to adopt an alternative style in response to a particular issue or situation.

A Final Note

The guidelines recommended here are designed to create a committee role that focuses on policy objectives and organizational strategies in academic affairs. Committees which have historically been relatively inactive or uninvolved may find that the "start-up costs" are considerable. Some administrators and faculty members might be unsettled by the committee's more active interest in academic affairs, and the staff work and data analyses required to fulfill some of these guidelines may tax the administration, especially at institutions where active boards and strategic planning are new phenomena. The Academic Affairs Committee must be sensitive to these possibilities and should move cautiously and diplomatically, but with purpose.

CHAPTER III

Academic Personnel Policy and Administration

RICHARD P. CHAIT

The academic programs of colleges and universities largely reflect (or should) an institution's mission, and the quality of the faculty members largely determines how well that mission is fulfilled. When from time to time the top institutions, schools, and departments are surveyed and ranked, the judgments are primarily assessments of the caliber of the faculty.

The faculty's importance to an institution's reputation might be reason enough to consider carefully academic policies and practices. There is also a powerful economic argument. Faculty compensation and related instructional expenses consume the lion's share of an institution's budget. A decision to tenure a 35-year-old faculty member will probably cost more than $1 million by the time the professor retires.

In today's environment personnel decisions will be critical and mistakes costly. With the end of the growth era it has become more difficult to maintain staffing flexibility just when it is most needed to facilitate curriculum flexibility. As the opportunity to change people and thus programs diminishes, each personnel decision assumes added significance and the cost of each mistake becomes magnified.

For this reason, the Academic Affairs Committee must be particularly attentive to faculty personnel policies and procedures, including such considerations as employment security, academic freedom, incentive structures, performance appraisal, and professional development.

Data Base: A Place to Begin

Nearly all colleges and universities recognize the need to manage their physical and fiscal resources. Capital and operating budgets are developed routinely, and fiscal projections are often made for five and ten year periods. Nearly all boards receive on an annual basis a balance sheet and a statement of changes in fund balances. But very few boards receive comparable information about academic personnel.

Planning for management of faculty resources might begin with an inventory of current staff. For example, the data might be arrayed by (1) department or school, (2) age, (3) sex, (4) race, (5) salary, (6) workload, (7) tenure status, (8) degree attainment, and (9) retirement date. There are a number of computer programs that facilitate simulation exercises. One can, for example, manipulate the policy variables that affect faculty flow, such as rates of tenure and promotion, length of probationary periods, retrenchment plans, compensation, retirement policies, and voluntary attrition.

Using these models, a college can ascertain the likely effects of contemplated policy changes. Fundamental analyses can be undertaken with regard to policies such as promotion, tenure, workload, and retirement. An automated faculty data base can answer questions such as:

• How many mandatory retirements will occur in each of the next ten years? What is the probability of voluntary retirement at age sixty and each year thereafter?

• As an annual average, what percent of the faculty, by

tenure status and rank, depart voluntarily? (At smaller institutions absolute numbers are likely to be more informative than percentages.)

• What percent of faculty members appointed in the same year reach the tenure decision, and among those faculty members, what percent earn tenure? (Again, at smaller institutions absolute numbers are likely to be more informative than percentages.) What would be the effects on turnover if that number were increased or decreased by ten percent?

• What is the average length of time between promotion from one rank to another? What would be the effect on the payroll if that number were increased or decreased by a year?

Throughout this chapter we will identify data elements that should be available to the Academic Affairs Committee to enlighten discussions, inform decisions, and indicate results. As a general proposition, we would recommend that the committee, in concert with the president and provost, ensure that the institution maintain, at a minimum, an academic personnel data base and that the administration regularly present to the committee summary analyses that emphasize significant changes and trends.

Few decisions can be wise in the absence of pertinent information, and few trustees can be enlightened in the absence of a regular flow of appropriate data.

Academic Tenure

(Portions of the material that follows first appeared in "Setting Tenure and Personnel Policies," by Richard P. Chait, Chapter Eleven of *The Handbook of College and University Trusteeship*, Richard T. Ingram and Associates. San Francisco: Jossey-Bass, 1980.)

Among personnel policies and actions, none looms larger than academic tenure. Despite tenure's central importance, many academicians and trustees alike are confused about the provisions and purposes of tenure policy. This confusion, in turn, adds to the larger controversy over the value and wisdom of a tenure system.

A definition might help to minimize the confusion. The

Keast Commission on Academic Tenure, cosponsored by the American Association of University Professors and the Association of American Colleges (1973), defined tenure as "an arrangement under which faculty appointments in an institution of higher education are continued until retirement for age or physical disability, subject to dismissal for adequate cause or unavoidable termination on account of financial exigency or change of institutional program" (p. 256). It must be remembered, however, that this is only a general definition and does not supersede policy provisions adopted by a board of trustees, enacted by a legislature, or negotiated by a faculty union.

Academic tenure will be neither more nor less than what official institutional policy stipulates, a principle underscored by the Bloomfield College case, 322 A.2d 846 (1974); *affirmed*, 346 A.2d 615 (1975). Throughout the decision, the court referred to the self-imposed limitations defined by college policy. "*By their choice of preconditions. . .* that the board's action be demonstrably bona fide . . . . Bearing in mind . . . the extremely severe restrictions *which the college has accepted on its authority to act. . . .* The actions of Bloomfield College with respect to the tenured status of its faculty members . . . overflowed the limits of its authority *as defined by its own policies*." (Emphases added.)

Three years later, in *Lumpert v. University of Dubuque*, 255 N.W.2d 168 (1977), the Iowa Supreme Court ruled similarly. "How restricted is the university's flexibility of course depends on the contract language used in regard to tenure. . . . Each case is subject to its own contractual provisions." The principle also extends to "financial exigency." In *Scheuer v. Creighton University*, 260 N.W. 2d 595 (1977) the Supreme Court of Nebraska declared, "We specifically hold the term financial exigency *as used in the contract of employment herein* may be limited to a financial exigency in a department or college." (Emphases added.)

Tenure aims to safeguard academic freedom and ensure a measure of economic security. Academic freedom has three essential components:

1. The freedom to conduct and publish research.

2. The freedom to teach and discuss issues pertinent to the course or subjects without introducing into the classroom irrelevant matters.

3. The freedom to speak or write as a citizen without speaking or writing expressly on behalf of the institution unless authorized to do so.

Unlike academic freedom, economic security is a well established and easily understood concept. By carefully specifying the grounds and procedures whereby tenured personnel may be dismissed, tenure protects against arbitrary and capricious personnel actions, thus providing significant job security.

It can also be argued that tenure benefits the institution as well as the individual. Traditionally, it has been held that tenure creates an environment that encourages faculty to undertake long-term and often high-risk projects. Second, the presence of a tenured faculty helps develop a coterie of professionals loyal to the institution yet sufficiently secure to act as constructive critics. Finally, and perhaps most important, the very nature of a tenure decision presumably forces the institution to assess each candidate carefully and thus exercise quality control.

Today academic tenure operates on almost all college campuses. About 85 percent of all colleges and universities have a tenure system, and these institutions employ about 95 percent of all full-time faculty. All universities, nearly all four year colleges, and some two-thirds of all two year colleges have a tenure system. In the institutions that have tenure systems, not all faculty have tenure. Nationwide, about 63.5 percent, (some 251,000 of the 457,000 full-time faculty) are tenured. Although criteria and procedures for awarding tenure differ from college to college, and even from school to school within a university, there are enough common elements to construct a generalized description of the bases and processes that govern tenure decisions. Normally, a faculty member automatically becomes a candidate for tenure at a prescribed moment, generally one year prior to the expiration of the probationary period. Denial of tenure almost always means that the unsuccessful candidate must leave the institution after a terminal year's contact—a provision referred to as the "up or out" rule.

Tenure decisions typically reflect assessments of performance and judgments about potential. Minimum eligibility requirements usually include:

Service in a probationary period. Normally three to seven years—although exceptions exist at both ends of this range—the probationary period offers the faculty member an opportunity to develop and refine the skills necessary for the position, and it offers the institution a chance to observe and evaluate the faculty member's work. Service elsewhere may be counted toward fulfillment of the probationary period, although credit for prior service usually may not exceed half the total probationary period.

Attainment of appropriate academic credentials. This would usually mean attaining the highest degree, such as a Ph.D. or D.B.A., normally awarded in one's field or discipline. Appointment to tenure without the terminal degree has become more and more the exception.

Appointment to an appropriate academic rank. Most commonly, faculty must hold or be qualified to hold the rank of assistant or associate professor. In a few instances, instructors are eligible for tenure.

Successful past performance. This is normally assessed in three broad areas: teaching, scholarship (or research), and community service. Of course, depending upon the institution or even the department, these criteria are weighted differently.

Growth potential. An individual's ability to continue to develop as a teacher and scholar is also considered. Most often, these forecasts are based upon the value colleagues attach to work done thus far by the faculty member.

Institutional needs. Increasingly and necessarily, colleges and universities consider candidates for tenure within the larger context of institutional needs. Personnel decisions, like budgetary decisions, must be linked to institutional priorities. Through strategic planning (discussed in Chapter I) and program reviews (see Chapter IV), most colleges and universities should be able to avoid a circumstance in which a faculty member on the threshold of a tenure decision learns that his or her particular discipline is no longer consistent with the plans of the institution. Common decency alone demands that there be fair notice.

Although tenure decisons unavoidably contain a subjective element, a substantial body of evidence is usually assembled to inform the deliberations. A typical dossier might include letters from outside references addressing the quality of the candidate's scholarship; the candidate's publications and scholarly reviews of these works; student evaluations of teaching; course syllabi; and, perhaps, a self-evaluation that includes the candidate's goals. If institutional needs are to be integral to the decision, then pertinent data on mission, enrollments, finances, faculty flow, tenure levels, and affirmative action should be furnished as well. Some colleges, such as St. Olaf, require that each department develop a long-range plan that serves as a backdrop for consideration of tenure candidates.

As a matter of procedure, the review process typically entails a sequence of deliberations and recommendations, often beginning at the departmental or program level. At many universities and some liberal arts colleges, the recommendations of department members, department chairpersons, and other colleagues carry great weight. Beyond the department, the process moves to the dean, a school-wide committee, a college or university-wide committee, the academic vice president, and the president. In many cases, the president eventually places a recommendation for action before the board of trustees; on some campuses tenure decisions come to the board only as a matter of information.

Establishing Tenure Policy

Academic tenure can engage a governing board at two levels: tenure policy and tenure decisions. A board should recognize that tenure policies must be set within a larger institutional context.

More concretely, the board must achieve a working knowledge of the following six items and how they interrelate: (1) existing bylaws, rules, regulations, and relevant statutes; (2) contracts and negotiated agreements, especially those that directly affect staffing patterns; (3) the institution's affirmative action plan; (4) the institution's budget; (5) the institution's mission statement and priorities; and (6) a profile of the institution's faculty as described earlier.

What tenure-related policies should the Academic Affairs Committee review periodically? With substantial participation by the college community, the committee should ensure that the *criteria* upon which tenure decisions are based are appropriate and pertinent. Some questions toward that end might include:

Does the probationary period provide adequate time to judge a faculty member's performance? Would more time be helpful? Would less time reduce anxieties?

Are assignments sufficiently varied during the probationary period to test a faculty member's abilities in all areas of responsibility? Or is the probationary period really one year's experience repeated six times?

Are the degree requirements appropriate to today's marketplace? How often are exceptions made?

Is the relative importance attached to teaching, research, and service consonant with the institution's mission? Is there sufficient latitude to accommodate faculty with different interests and strengths?

Are institutional need and affirmative action recognized as criteria? If so, how? If not, why not?

What policy statements do faculty receive? How are standards and expectations communicated to the faculty? Have they changed in the last 5-10 years?

Trustees should recognize that, especially at large universities, different departments, schools, and colleges may have different emphases, standards, and expectations. Conformity to the institution's central mission does not necessarily require uniformity on all aspects of tenure policies and criteria. Trustees would be well advised to leave to faculty and academic administrators matters of detail in the criteria for tenure. The relative importance of refereed versus nonrefereed journals, the significance of coauthorship of articles, the relative importance of peer review of teaching versus student evaluations, are not matters for trustee considerations. The principal role of the Academic Affairs Committee should be to ensure that the general criteria for tenure are clearly stated, widely available, and supportive of the institution's mission.

From time to time some colleges and universities might entertain changes in the fundamental provisions of academic tenure. For example, there might be a proposal to establish a tenure quota or a nontenure track, or to extend the probationary period. These are potentially explosive issues; trustees should proceed with caution. Where the impetus for change comes from within the board or from the legislature, the focus should be on the policy objective. The faculty and administration should determine the best means to a specified end.

With respect to the process employed to reach tenure decisions, the board should ascertain that procedures are reasonable, comprehensible, and appropriate to the organization's structure. As a check, an Academic Affairs Committee might ask the administration to "walk" the committee through the process. En route, members might ask such questions as:

• What documents do faculty receive that explain the process?

• Does the process allow an evaluative record to be constructed from the start of the probationary period?

• How do the procedures provide faculty with due process?

• Are the procedures acceptable and usable to a large majority of the campus community?

• Are there major differences in procedures across academic units of the institution? If so, why?

Once again, the committee's role is not to write procedures. It is to ensure that there are procedures that are widely understood and appropriate to the task.

Making Tenure Decisions

Tenure decisions require sophisticated assessments of the candidates' professional abilities, assessments best rendered by peers. Yet, tenure decisions also require familiarity with institutional needs and priorities. If trustees are to review tenure decisions at all, the primary focus should be on the "fit" between individual merit, as judged by academic professions, and institutional needs, as judged by the academic administration and the board.

With perspective focused on institutional needs, a board or Academic Affairs Committee might ask such questions as:

• Do we have the financial resources to support these appointments over the long term?

• Are these permanent appointments consistent with the school's long-term objectives, curriculum needs, and affirmative action plans?

• Will these decisions unwisely constrain institutional flexibility or unduly bind a particular department?

• Do enrollment and placement patterns warrant a permanent appointment?

• Will these decisions foreclose even more attractive appointments to tenure within the foreseeable future?

• If tenure were denied, where would the dollars saved be allocated—to the same position, another program, a different department?

These questions suggest the kind of data that a board requires to participate effectively in tenure decisions and, for that matter, to review tenure policies. Too often, administrators furnish to boards the very same information provided to faculty and deans even though trustees have (or should have) a different set of concerns. If trustees receive only information about the individual merit of each candidate, how can the board help but dwell on that aspect of each decision? If, however, the board receives information on departmental plans, institutional priorities, affirmative action, and financial conditions, a very different discussion may ensue. Attention will be directed more to broad issues of staffing and planning than to a review of candidates' qualifications on a case-by-case basis.

If the Academic Affairs Committee feels assured by the president or the chief academic officer that the prescribed process has been followed and the appropriate criteria applied, it should rarely have cause to review individual tenure recommendations in depth. As an instructional exercise, however, the committee might examine dossiers from years past to stimulate a faculty review committee and thus learn firsthand about the difficult (or easy) decisions tenure cases pose.

While a board might occasionally be tempted to investigate the merits of a recommendation from the president that has created controversy on campus, the board should limit review only to those cases that present a question of violation of college policy or procedure. Unless state government policy or a local labor contract stipulate otherwise, a board should not serve as a court of last resort for a faculty member refused tenure after established policies and procedures have been equitably applied. A review on merit by the board will very likely be perceived as an assault on faculty autonomy, a failure to support the president, or both.

In certain cases, institutional bylaws, state policy, or a labor contract may require that, upon petition, the board review a tenure decision or hear a grievance. Boards affected by such conditions should have guidelines that include the following:

1. Assertion of the board's authority to render a final decision.

2. Establishment of a review procedure that assures due process and respects confidentiality.

3. Assignment of the responsibility for review to the Academic Affairs Committee.

4. Prescription of the range of sanctions and remedies that can be applied.

5. Description of the general circumstances, such as a charge of unlawful discrimination, under which the board might consider questions of individual merit.

Prior to any review, the board should consult legal counsel on such matters as due process, need for transcripts, rules of evidence, and personal liability.

Tenure Policy Audit

Periodically, the Academic Affairs Committee should receive data on the operation and effectiveness of the college's tenure system. The data should reveal:

• What percentage of a faculty cohort (professors appointed in the same year) reach the point of tenure decision? What percentage has been previously eliminated? What percentage resigned and why? (To reiterate, at smaller institutions absolute numbers are likely to be more informative than percentages.)

• Of those considered for the tenure decision, what percentage were successful?

• How many tenure decisions lead to a grievance on process? On substance? What has been the outcome?

In reviewing the data, the committee might ask:

• Are there any marked differences in selectivity among academic units? If so, why?

• Are there any marked differences between the success rates of women and minorities and other faculty members?

• Does tenure appear to be more or less difficult to obtain than a few years ago? What does that trend suggest? (A higher success rate could mean, among other things, that the college is attracting better faculty or, conversely, relaxing standards.)

The committee might also wish to review data on institutional flexibility. Typically, the board wants to know the institution's tenure level. Some prior questions might be:

• How is the tenure ratio calculated?

• What personnel categories are included in the denominator?

• Are part-time faculty, adjunct faculty, administrators, graduate students, librarians, coaches, and counselors included?

The numerator should be the number of tenured faculty;

the denominator should be the numerator plus the number of nontenured, tenure-eligible faculty. The data should answer such questions as:

• What percentage of the instructional payroll is committed to tenured faculty?

• What percentage of the faculty are not on the tenure track?

• What percent of the faculty, by 5-10 year age groupings, hold tenure?

• What is the projected tenure level 3, 5, and 10 years from now, given current success rates and retirement rates?

These data are not indicators of quality or even surrogate measures of quality. On the other hand, such information will help an Academic Affairs Committee and a board of trustees better understand faculty flow patterns, personnel needs, and staffing plans. Perhaps more important, the data should invite and provoke a discussion of the effectiveness of the tenure systems and whether the institution's objectives are being met.

Reductions in Force

Some academicians argue that institutions should not develop policies to terminate faculty members and eliminate faculty positions unless and until the policies are needed. Otherwise, the very effort to establish retrenchment policies will arouse suspicion and harm morale. After all, the faculty will reason, why would a college develop retrenchment policies unless the administration expected to use them?

The author disagrees with that view, and recommends that institutions draft retrenchment policies and procedures in advance of their need. An atmosphere of crisis is not conducive to formulation of policy, least of all retrenchment policy. The absence of urgency affords the campus community the opportunity to deliberate and to fashion policy without concern for the immediate impact on particular individuals.

The Academic Affairs Committee might, on occasion, have to prompt the campus community to develop retrenchment policies and a contingency plan. Some campuses are understandably reluctant to confront the issues associated with retrenchment. The most logical place to start would be with the simplest questions: Do we have policies that govern reduction of the faculty work force? If not, when will such policies be formulated? From these basic questions, other lines of inquiry flow.

The Academic Affairs Committee might wish to discuss with faculty representatives and academic administrators whether there are certain *principles* of retrenchment that must prevail. These principles, developed with substantial faculty involvement, should precede the formulation of policy details. Should tenure status be held inviolate? Should the burden of layoffs be selectively or equally distributed? Should faculty be terminated with the least adverse effect on affirmative action or on seniority?

As a rule, principles that promote selective choices consonant with an overall institutional strategy should be preferred. Across-the-board cutbacks based solely on seniority are not consistent with that objective. In any case, retrenchment policies should address seven central considerations, and for each area we suggest some questions members of the Academic Affairs Committee might ask.

1. *Locus of tenure*. Do faculty members hold tenure in a department, a program, a college, or a university? The answer to that question will signficantly influence the options available to an institution that must retrench. If faculty hold tenure at the college and not in a department it could affect the university's capacity to lay off personnel on a programmatic basis.

2. *Entitlements of tenure*. What rights and privileges will be accorded faculty members adversely affected by retrenchment decisions? Do faculty enjoy the right to be relocated within the university? To be retrained? If so, at whose expense and over what period of time? To receive severance pay? What constitutes "due notice"? Trustees should remember that these decisions, like most other personnel policies, are within the university's province to determine (absent any relevant state statutes or collective bargain-

ing agreements).

3. *Grounds for termination*. What will be acceptable grounds for terminating faculty through retrenchment? In general, colleges and universities cite two circumstances that may trigger retrenchment.

A. *Financial exigency* is a somewhat imprecise term that conveys a degree of financial hardship. Institutional policy should add clarity and specificity to the term. Among the issues to be resolved are these: Should the board alone have the authority to declare and end financial exigency? Should financial exigency be defined as chronic financial difficulties or as an acute financial emergency? Should the term be limited to operating budgets and deficits? Can the endowment be preserved (and augmented) and capital construction undertaken once an exigency has been declared? Should policy permit exigency to be limited to a program or a department or should the term apply only to circumstances where the institution as a whole faces imminent insolvency?

These policy questions juxtapose and directly affect matters of institutional flexibility and employment security. As a first step toward a policy statement that strikes a balance appropriate to local conditions, the Academic Affairs Committee should consult the AAUP's recommended regulations (1977, revised, 1981) and Furniss's (1976) critique of the AAUP's general position.

B. *Program discontinuation*. A college or university might elect to eliminate a program or a department for reasons unrelated or only indirectly related to finances. The motivation can, for example, be a matter of academic quality, a shift of program emphases, or a lack of sufficient enrollments.

Policies on program discontinuation should answer these questions: What constitutes a "program"? Is it a sequence of courses? An area of study? A department? Must the "problem" be long-range or might it be cyclical? Must the reasons for discontinuation be "essentially educational" (AAUP 1977) or can there be a mix of educational and financial considerations? A policy on program discontinuation should identify the criteria for a review of program quality, the process, and the range of alternatives such as reduction, consolidation, or transfer of programs.

4. *Criteria for termination.* The policy should make clear *who* holds the authority to terminate faculty. What criteria are to be applied and are they to be weighted or rank-ordered? Among the criteria that can be included are: past performance, potential, compatibility with program needs, enrollment histories and projections, academic credentials, tenure status, and seniority. Faculty, administrators, and trustees alike should recognize that the choice and relative significance of these criteria rests with the institution. Even the definition of seniority, which can be defined by length of service, rank, salary, tenure status, or some combination thereof, should be determined locally.

5. *Replacement.* A retrenchment policy should delineate those circumstances, if any, where the institution might terminate faculty in one area and hire faculty in another area. Will terminated faculty members have the right of first refusal when positions are restored? For how long will those "recall rights" extend?

6. *Appeals process.* Any retrenchment policy should provide an opportunity for due process. At a *minimum*, due process includes: (a) a written explanation of the reason or reasons for terminating faculty; (b) a written description of the manner in which that decision was reached; (c) a "reasonable disclosure" of the information that decision makers used; and (d) an opportunity for terminated faculty to have a hearing or "fair showing," which is a chance to argue that the decision was arbitrary, capricious, or unlawful. (See *Johnson v. Board of Regents of University of Wisconsin System*, 377 F. Supp. 227, 1974.)

7. *Policy alternatives.* Termination of faculty members need not be the only response to financial distress or program changes. There are alternatives such as pay reductions, workload reductions, transfer to other programs or departments, retraining, and early or phased retirement. Whether separately or as a part of an overall retrenchment plan, the availability of these options should be detailed.

With respect to retrenchment, then, trustees should ensure that a policy has been developed with ample faculty participation. The Academic Affairs Committee should review current policies or policy drafts to make certain that the seven key elements of a retrenchment policy are addressed adequately and unambiguously.

The trustees' role does not end there. The board should encourage and, if need be, direct the administration to initiate strategies and approaches that will make retrenchment less likely or even unnecessary. Some of these strategies are described more fully in other chapters. For now, suffice it to say that some preventive measures might include:

1. Strategic plans. The process generally entails an assessment of people, programs, and prospects and an effort to match internal strengths with external opportunities.

2. Salary reductions or slowed rates of pay increases. Payroll represents the greatest expense and each salary increase adds cumulatively to the base.

3. External program reviews. Every 5-7 years each program or department might be evaluated by a team of outside experts. The review panel might consider program leadership, faculty quality, prospects for external support, student demand, student placement, financial requirements for program improvement, and cost effectiveness.

4. "Distant early warning signals." Institutions can establish any number of warning signals that would precipitate "heightened scrutiny" of a department. Among the trip wires that might trigger reviews are the patterns of (and relationship among) student enrollment, faculty manpower, income and expense, and program costs of a department versus a college or university-wide average.

5. Reductions and reallocations through some process such as zero-based budgeting, management by objectives, or planning, programming, and budgeting systems. The aims are to adjust incrementally through measures such as management of attrition, control of position vacancies, nonrenewal of appointments,

reallocation of resources, or "taxes" or levies against a department or school.

6. Search for new resources through tactics such as entrepreneurship, contract research, differentiated fees, increased workloads, new markets, cooperative programs, shared appointments with other colleges, and fund raising. A focus on retrenchment must not blind the institution to opportunities for expanding the resource base or more effective use of current resources. On that score, trustees can lead the way through probing and prodding.

Compensation

Faculty compensation can be divided into two categories: salary and benefits. Salary encompasses the direct remuneration for regular assignments, overload, and special stipends attached, for example, to named professorships and endowed chairs. Benefits include life, health, and disability insurance, sick leave, vacations, pensions, and tuition remission.

Compensation plans for faculty can serve various purposes. The Academic Affairs Committee should ask faculty and administrative representatives which goals are paramount and whether the policy objectives are satisfied. Some typical policy goals together with measures of the effectiveness of the policy follow.

1. *Equity*. Presumably salary should reflect performance, rank, length of service, and other work-related criteria. Salary should not be determined by sex, race, religious background, or age (except as a surrogate measure of experience and length of service). The AAUP has developed a salary evaluation kit designed to ascertain if any unlawful salary discrimination exists. The Academic Affairs Committee should ask that such analyses be conducted and the results reported to the committee.

2. *Merit*. Many institutions allocate at least some salary increase money for "merit," based on an evaluation of performance. Merit pay, as a practice, can be controversial since the recipients of less than average increases are likely to question the objectivity

of the evaluation. In addition, some academics dislike in principle a system that provides rewards for some at the cost of punishment for others.

A decision to adopt merit pay should require board concurrence, and the Academic Affairs Committee should periodically review with the administration the process and criteria used to determine merit. There should be some evidence that salary decisions correlate with performance appraisals. At a college-wide or university-wide level, the committee might ask for salary distribution curves. On the assumption that not all faculty perform equally, the committee should expect a fairly uneven distribution of raises. The administraton might survey faculty now and then on the fairness and appropriateness of the merit system and make known the results.

3. *Competitiveness*. Compensation should be at a level sufficient to attract and retain talented faculty. The committee might ask the administration to monitor voluntary turnover and to conduct exit interviews (or administer questionnaires) that would reveal the degree to which valued professors are leaving due primarily to economic considerations. Similar information could be obtained from faculty who are offered appointments at the college and decline the invitation.

At the level of departments or colleges, institutions can compare compensation packages with counterparts elsewhere. There are national surveys, such as the AAUP's, or peer surveys, such as the Association of American Universities (AAU) Data Exchange. The key consideration is to select institutions that both the faculty and the administration regard as comparable.

4. *Ability to pay*. No organization can afford for long to offer salaries that exceed its ability to pay. Through consultation with the administration and the Finance Committee of the board, the Academic Affairs Committee should determine whether payroll represents an appropriate portion of expenses and a reasonable expenditure as measured absolutely.

5. *Incentive to motivate*. Do people work better for the

prospect of more pay? One can find research to support all sides of the argument, but it appears doubtful that the prospect of pay increases alone will significantly motivate faculty performance. (Lawler 1971)

Most studies of academics suggest that intrinsic satisfactions are more important than extrinsic rewards (e.g., McKeachie 1979). In any case, one approach would be to poll faculty periodically on questions pertinent to pay satisfaction and the effect, if any, of pay as a motivating force.

The committee and the board more generally should participate in discussions and decisions about the relative priority of these five policy objectives. The committee should also request that on a regular basis data be collected and reports provided that convey some measure of the effects and effectiveness of the college's compensation policies.

The Academic Affairs Committee and the board might also review administrative decisions on various policy options. Among those a college or university might consider are:

• Whether to provide all employees with the same coverage or to allow cafeteria-style benefits where each person chooses, up to a fixed dollar limit, a package of benefits suited to that individual's needs.

• Whether all salary increases should be folded into a base salary or whether some one-time payments, bonuses, and prizes should be allowed or encouraged.

• Whether there should be fewer faculty positions, greater workloads, and higher salaries.

• Whether or to what extent salaries should take into account staffing shortages and surpluses.

• Whether salaries should be public or confidential.

• Whether workload (and salaries) should be adjusted to increase opportunities for outside earnings.

One other role for the Academic Affairs Committee extends beyond salary and benefits to the broader area of incentives. It should ensure that the administration does not overlook the realm of nonsalary rewards such as travel funds, library and laboratory support, smaller classes, honors sections, secretarial help, research assistants, more convenient schedules, and new faculty positions. Nor should the college underestimate the value some faculty attach to such nonmonetary rewards as publicity, praise, recognition— even the opportunity to meet with trustees.

Faculty Evaluation

Students, colleagues, and administrators continuously evaluate faculty much as faculty evaluate students, administrators, and one another. The threshold questions concern: (1) whether the evaluations should be formal and systematic or informal and casual; and (2) what purposes the evaluations should serve.

Prior to the tenure decision, formal evaluations of faculty members are rather standard procedures. Typically, probationary faculty members are evaluated annually or perhaps every other year in some generally systematic fashion. The tenure decision represents (or should) a comprehensive culmination of these earlier assessments. Subsequent to the tenure decision, evaluation practices vary greatly. Some institutions do not formally evaluate tenured faculty; most others do so only in conjunction with salary, promotion, or other personnel decisions. While not yet a widespread practice, periodic, formal evaluations of tenured faculty members appears to be on the increase.

Many faculty members argue that the normal course of events on campus provides all the evaluation data needed to assess the performance of tenured faculty. There are, for example, reviews of faculty sabbatical proposals, decisions by publishers and refereed journals, critiques by reviewers, determinations by funding agencies, salary assessments by department heads, and course evaluations by students.

At strong colleges and universities with well-established traditions of rigorous self-regulation, these mechanisms might suffice. At schools without these traditions and with less external review of faculty scholarship, a more systematic post-tenure evaluation policy might be warranted. And even at the finest colleges and universities, regular reviews can be a constructive supplement to the other assessments.

It is noteworthy that the participants at a 1983 conference on Evaluation of Tenured Faculty, cosponsored by the AAUP and the American Council on Education, described the evaluation of tenured faculty members "on a continuing basis, formal and informal" as "healthy and indeed valuable." The conferees recommended that "written descriptions of the purposes, criteria and methods by which these evaluations are made should be provided to faculty." Trustees should be furnished the same information.

The purposes of evaluations can be categorized as either summative or formative. Summative evaluations inform personnel decisions. They are intended to: (1) contribute to fair and informed promotion and tenure decisions; (2) enlighten decisions on the distribution of such rewards as salary increases and sabbatical leaves; and (3) establish a historical record that could lead to the termination of faculty members unable to remedy major shortcomings in performance. (The AAUP/ACE conferees recommended that post-tenure evaluations "not be used as a ground to dismiss tenured faculty." Should informal resolution fail, the conferees advised that "existing due process procedures" be employed.) Formative evaluations, on the other hand, are intended principally to benefit the person under review. These evaluations, which will probably be more descriptive than judgmental, should advance the faculty member's professional growth and development. Formative evaluations might lead, for example, to changes in lecture style or research agendas.

As a rule, summative and formative evaluations should be separate processes. One evaluation can rarely serve both purposes. The Academic Affairs Committee should be a party to discussion of the policy objectives of faculty evaluation and the relative emphasis to be placed on summative and formative reviews.

With respect to summative evaluations, the committee should periodically review and discuss with faculty and administrators the areas to be assessed. Typically these are: instructional and advising activities, research and scholarship, and service to the university, the community, and the profession. As discussed earlier, some colleges add a fourth category, the match between the individual's talents and the organization's needs.

At comprehensive "multiversities" the relative priority assigned to each area can differ by department, school, or college. By contrast, the priorities at liberal arts and community colleges are probably more consistent, if not uniform. In any case, the concern should be whether the areas and the relative priorities for faculty evaluation are consonant with the institution's mission.

Selection of the specific criteria, standards, and sources of evidence for performance appraisals should rest with the faculty, although the faculty's decisions and departmental policy statements should be available and comprehensible to the committee. For the sake of faculty as well as trustees, the committee might properly ask the president to ensure that each academic unit prepare a written description of the substance and process of faculty evaluation.

The committee might ask:
- What are the paramount purposes of faculty evaluation?
- What areas are evaluated and what criteria are applied? Do these differ by department, school, or college? If so, why?
- How are criteria and standards communicated to the faculty?
- Are the standards based on performance relative to others or relative to the achievement of certain objectives?
- Is the evidence pertinent to the areas under review, germane to the individual's assignment, and offered by persons qualified to judge?
- Who participates in the evaluation? What role, if any, do students, peers, administrators, and outside experts play?
- How often do evaluations occur? Are all faculty (and administrators) evaluated regularly? If not, why are certain groups excluded?

• How are the results used? Are evaluations and rewards closely correlated?

• Who "manages" the process and the data? How are faculty informed of the results?

To summarize, the chief roles of the Academic Affairs Committee in evaluation are to participate in decisions about the purposes and areas of evaluation, and to ensure that the faculty develops appropriate criteria, standards, and sources of evidence. Aside from reviewing policy statements, the committee from time to time might want to examine some performance appraisals. (The file should be edited or altered to preclude identification of the person under review.) Do these assessments at least differentiate among the superior, satisfactory, and unsatisfactory performers? Now and then the committee should also meet with faculty representatives to determine whether the faculty has participated in the development of evaluation policies and to determine whether the faculty finds the process fair, credible, and valid.

Finally, the committee should recognize that evaluation requires leadership by example. Do the committee and the board have an evaluation system for their members and work that would meet the tests applied to faculty evaluation schemes?

Faculty Development

Faculty development will become increasingly important as faculty mobility becomes increasingly constrained. Most goals an institution hopes to achieve in the next few years will probably have to be attained by the faculty now in place. Just as deferred maintenance of facilities can lead to major difficulties, so too can deferred maintenance of faculty.

Much as other personnel policies we have discussed, the pivotal issue concerns policy objectives; the committee's attention should be directed to that aspect of faculty development. Broadly defined, faculty development programs can be divided into three categories.

Some faculty development activities are considered

elements of the reward structure with opportunities earned by past performance and perceived potential. In these instances, faculty development leads to sabbaticals, research leaves, reduced workloads, professional conferences, new courses, colloquia, and the like. Other programs are conceived as a way to overcome deficiencies among inadequate professors. These programs lead to additional training, diagnostic activities, remedial workshops, tutoring, mentoring, and early retirement.

Still other programs are designed as a means to retrain faculty members, often in undersubscribed programs, for assignment in areas with greater student demand. Such efforts might entail career counseling, additional coursework, attachment to a "faculty mentor," or an "internship" in another department.

Note that these approaches to faculty development serve very different purposes, probably involve different members of the faculty, and represent different priorities for the use of scarce resources. The committee might discuss with faculty and staff whether to have a formal faculty development program and, if so, what the dominant policy objective should be.

There are other choices to be made at the operational level, and while these matters need not engage the committee directly, it might wish to review the decisions reached by the faculty and staff and the rationales for these decisions. Among the more crucial policy options are:

• Whether faculty development is to be a centrally funded, steadily supported activity or a program supported largely and irregularly by grants and gifts.

• Whether the program is to be overseen largely by faculty and based on competitive proposals or is to be controlled by the administration.

• Whether the program will be developed around a broad range of activities from which faculty may choose or around a narrow range of prescribed activities to which faculty can be assigned.

• Whether the program is to be based on self-determined professional roles and activities or on perceived problems of individuals and the needs of organizations.

Now and then, the Academic Affairs Committee might request a report on faculty development. The data should provide: (1) participation rates by school, department, and college by type of activity and tenure; (2) a summary of activities undertaken and the results; and (3) a summary of the costs.

The committee should not be concerned with approving specific faculty development activities; these decisions are the proper province of the faculty and the academic administration. On some campuses, approval of sabbatical leaves might be an exception. Here too, however, the committee might focus more profitably on the development of a rigorous peer review process rather than on consideration of each sabbatical proposal.

To gain some sense of the breadth and range of faculty interests, the committee and the board might request an annual informational report on sabbatical activities.

Summary

Academic personnel policies extend well beyond the topics covered here. There are, for example, questions of promotion, workload, retirement, and outside employment. Not all of these issues can be addressed in a single chapter and perhaps not even in a single volume. We have selected those topics likely to be of greatest concern to the Academic Affairs Committee.

Despite the variety and number of academic personnel policies, we believe that policy formulation on all these issues can be approached in a similar manner. Above all else, the committee's participation and discussions should focus on policy objectives. Once the policy objectives have been determined, the administration in concert with the faculty should develop policy statements. The committee should review these policy statements, raise questions, probe rationales, and prompt reconsideration.

Finally, the effectiveness of a policy—the degree to which it attains the stated objectives—should be monitored by the administration and periodically reported, with corroborative data, to the committee. Changes in policy or personnel should be made as deemed necessary.

Sound personnel policies and procedures are neither a panacea nor a substitute for talented faculty and adequate resources. Poor policies or ineffective policy execution can, however, reduce motivation, provoke dissatisfaction, and waste human as well as fiscal resources. By contrast, well-reasoned and well-administered policies can help to create an overall environment that is conducive to bringing out the best in people.

CHAPTER IV

Academic Programs

KENNETH P. MORTIMER

Ⅰn overseeing the educational program, according to Corson, "trustees should review every six months or every year what new programs have been added [and] . . . dropped." (1980, p. 114). The ideal mechanism for such regular review is the Academic Affairs Committee. Guidelines and procedures should be developed in consultation with the faculty and administration.

This chapter has three major sections. The first part discusses the need for concern about academic programs, the second curriculum reform and general education, and the third program approval and review, accreditation, and program closure.

1. THE NEED FOR TRUSTEE OVERSIGHT

Since resources are scarce it is imperative that institutional effort not be squandered on programs that have lost their vitality.

Trustees need to be watchful so that continued or prolonged financial problems do not result in erosion of academic quality.

Student Interests

Perhaps the most difficult problem confronting trustees and administrators today is the recent shift in student demand from the more traditional liberal arts to career-oriented programs. From 1969 to 1976 undergraduate major enrollments in the professions rose from 38 to 58 percent of all majors whereas enrollment dropped from 9 to 5 percent in the humanities majors and from 18 to 12 percent in the social sciences. (Stadtman, 1980, pp. 26 and 59)

Some scholars explain part of this shift by reference to the "New Student," defined by K. Patricia Cross as "those who score in the lowest third on tests of academic ability."

> New students are positively attracted to careers and prefer to learn things that are tangible and useful.They tend not to value the academic model of higher education that is prized by faculty, preferring instead a vocational model that will teach them what they need to know to make a good living. (Cross, 1972, p. 159)

Pressures for more career-oriented programs permeate even the most selective liberal arts colleges. Students at these more traditional institutions often require or request substantial internship opportunities, more computer-based courses, the opportunity to pursue dual majors, and more complete career placement programs as a bridge between the liberal arts and the world of work. Changes in student interests and program requirements should be an essential concern of an Academic Affairs Committee.

Educational Programs and Institutional Strategy

Since no institutional strategy can be effective without a consideration of academic programs, trustees have yet another reason to oversee educational offerings. Here several points about strategies and strategic planning are relevant.

Program strength is a critical component of most definitions of institutional strategy. Any institution that seeks to develop an academic strategy must know its program *priorities*. Moreover, the strategic planning process and making strategic choices require institutions to link fiscal, personnel and academic priorities. This holistic view of the institution is a unique trustee and presidential responsibility.

Scientific and Technological Change

Relevant scientific and technological advances must be incorporated into the institution's programs. In some cases scientific and technological advances might require that trustees be prepared to help raise significant funds to repair, modify, or construct new facilities. In other cases a few trustees with expertise in technological areas might be able to help forecast and monitor new developments.

The rapid rise in computers and related technologies serves as a vivid example of scientific and technological changes and of the need to monitor academic programs. Trustees need to know how computers are being managed in the curriculum and whether lack of institutional resources or of faculty talent constitutes a serious barrier to student opportunity to gain exposure to computers.

In summary, when exercising their responsibilities for overseeing programs, trustees should seek answers to such questions as the following:

• What is the impact of any financial problems on the quality of the institution's programs?

• How has the institution adapted to changes in student preferences?

• How well do the institution's academic programs fit its overall strategy?

• What adaptations in academic programs have been made in response to new scientific and technological development?

• What are the implications of these changes for existing plant and facilities?

2. CURRICULUM REFORM

Trustees should be sensitive to the fact that faculty expertise might be limited to developments in the disciplines and that matters of general education and institutional program balance might not receive adequate attention. Therefore, questions about general education should be sensitive to the fact that no one model fits all institutions.

Trustees should seek answers to the following questions about general education and the institution's curriculum:

• What philosophies of education are reflected in the curriculum and are they consistent with the institution's mission?

• Is the balance between general education requirements, the major, and electives appropriate for the institution's mission, size, and curricular diversity?

• Are there minimum levels required in English language and mathematical skills?

• Are there special courses for nonmajors, or are introductory courses designed for those who intend to major in the field?

• Are courses available that provide for broad learning experiences that are assembled in an additive way around general themes like "Women's Role in Society" or "East Asian Civilization"?

• Is the faculty reward structure sufficiently flexible so that those interested in developing answers to these questions receive support and encouragement?

General education should be a source of special concern to trustees if there is evidence of long-term neglect.

When general education has been neglected for too long, the ills become so severe that they cannot be remedied by separate actions on the part of individual faculty members, however well-meaning. The program as a whole must be reviewed; the college must redefine its vision of the generally educated person and decide how the instructional program as a whole can foster the development of such a person. (Gaff, 1983, pp. pp. 107-108)

3. PROGRAM APPROVAL AND REVIEW

Institutional policy should require board approval to open a new program or close an existing one. Such decisions are fundamental to the institution's vitality and involve questions of finance, appropriateness to institutional mission and strategy, and the most effective use of resources. Clearly these issues require trustee attention.

Requests for new programs might be a natural extension of current student and faculty interests. In some cases, new faculty are hired precisely to develop programs.

Another source of new programs is the emergence of new knowledge or technology. While some of the pressures to reorganize departments stem from scientific advances in the traditional disciplines such as chemistry, physics, and biology, the most urgent demands have derived recently from the increased use of computers and computer technology.

Responsiveness to demonstrated community and/or student needs is another reason to develop new programs. Several community colleges and many regionally oriented four year colleges undertake periodic assessments to ensure that their program development reflects genuine community needs. Most institutions have had to respond with new programs to the general decline in student reading, writing, math, and study skills.

These reasons suggest a series of questions trustees should ask when considering whether to approve new programs.

• Is the program consistent with the institution's mission and strategic posture?

• How much will the program cost and how will these costs be met? Will it be more or less than existing programs? (See next chapter for additional questions about costs.)

• Is there reasonable evidence of student/community interest in or demand for the program, e.g., market surveys, student surveys or national developments?

• Is there reasonable evidence that the quality of faculty and prospective students is consistent with other programs in the institution?

• Will any special physical facilities or faculty expertise be needed that is not now available?

Review of Existing Programs

The discussion about institutional program review can be summarized around four basic questions.

1. What are the purposes of program review?
2. What process should be followed?
3. What criteria are relevant to the process?
4. What action should result from the review?

Purposes. While most program reviews are intended principally to improve the quality of academic programs, a review system usually will consider potential redistribution of resources and reductions in program commitment as well. At an institution satisfied with its current strategic posture and program configuration, the reviews would be designed chiefly to monitor program quality and assure continued vitality. At another institution where significant reductions, reallocations, and retrenchments are necessary, the program reviews can provide information essential to these decisions. In such cases there should be an understanding that the process is more likely to be controversial and conflict-ridden.

Process of Review. Program review is a six-step process.

1. A program self-study should precede the appointment of any review committee. The program being reviewed should be asked for answers to at least the following questions.

• What is your collective assessment of the program's current and future prospects?

• To what extent is the program consistent with the institution's mission and strategic posture?

• How does the program "match up" on the criteria (listed in Table 1) specified by the review process?

• What proposals for increased or decreased resources are appropriate and why?

• How can the quality of the program be improved?

2. A review committee should be appointed by the dean or other appropriate official when the self-study is well along or completed. It is possible that external consultants could be used at this stage in the process. The committee should review all material assembled for the self-study and judge the adequacy of the program's answers to the questions posed.

3. The committee should then write a formal report on its assessment and discuss the report with appropriate representatives of the unit under review. The report should have specific recommendations for improvements and/or modifications.

4. The administration and the trustees should act. In most cases the action will be to acknowledge the report and take it under consideration. But in cases where the data and recommendations provoke more substantive decisions, such as reduction or closure, the decisions and the rationales should be communicated directly to the committee and the unit.

5. A process should be developed to follow up on the progress made on any recommendations for improvement or other actions taken. In some cases the recommended action might be to review the program again within a year or two. In other cases the review might be scheduled again in accord with the institution's normal review cycle.

Criteria for Review. An institution must specify both for the self-study team and the evaluation committee the relevant criteria to apply. Table 1 suggests rating categories for each of these criteria. The intent here is *not* to arrive only at quantitative assessments; the information should be used to arrive at value judgments about decision alternatives based on both qualitative and quantitative data.

Trustees should be prepared to help administrators assign relative priorities to the criteria and make value judgments about the program's worth to their institution.

Before we turn to one possible result of these value

Criteria for Evaluation of Existing and Proposed Programs

Evaluative Criteria	Rating Categories		Program Clusters
QUALITY			
Quality of Faculty	Exceptional, Strong, Adequate, Weak		The programs to be continued at the current level of activity regarding resource allocation, enrollments, and number of faculty.
Quality of Student	High, Medium, Low		
Quality of Library Holdings	Excellent, Adequate, Insufficient		
Quality of Facilities & Equipment	Excellent, Adequate, Insufficient		
NEED		Evaluation of Individual Programs	
Centrality to Mission	Yes, No		Existing programs to be continued but at a reduced level of activity and resources.
Present Student Demand	High, Moderate, Low		
Projected Student Demand	Growing, Stable, Declining		
Demand for Graduates	High, Medium, Low		
Locational Advantage	Yes, No		
Comparative Advantage	Yes, No		
COST			
Cost/Revenue Relationship	Good, Adequate, Poor		Programs now in existence that are to be phased out. New programs to be developed.
Other Costs and Benefits	(Listing)		

Source: Robert C. Shirley and J. Fredericks Volkwein. "Establishing Academic Program Priorities." *Journal of Higher Education* 49 (September/October 1978): 478.

judgments, program closure, the special case of institutional and program reviews for accreditation needs to be discussed.

Accreditation. Voluntary accreditation is a system of nongovernmental, self-regulatory quality control that can be divided into two categories: institutional accrediting and specialized or programmatic accrediting. Institutional accrediting is conducted by six regional associations of colleges and schools and four national institutional accrediting bodies. Specialized accrediting is carried on by about forty national organizations concerned with professional study in such diverse fields as law, medicine, engineering, business, and nursing.

These accrediting bodies are an important element in maintaining a diverse set of postsecondary institutions with reasonable standards of quality and without excessive government regulation.

In order to educate its members and to determine how trustees can participate constructively in accreditation activities, AGB appointed a special subcommittee of its Public Policy Committee. The committee's report, *The Board's Role in Accreditation* (Association of Governing Boards, 1982), constitutes an important resource for trustees.

The report makes five recommendations for board participation in institutional accreditation:

1. Board members should be informed about and participate in accreditation activities along with faculty and administrators.

2. The board should actively participate in the institutional self-study.

3. The board should be informed of the objectives and activities of the visiting team.

4. The board or its representatives should meet with the visiting team.

5. The board should review and evaluate the final report, and help implement those recommendations it approves.

Specialized accreditation, because it involves reviews of specific programs, can require a different sort of trustee participation. The report's three recommendations can be paraphrased as follows:

• Trustees should be familar with the purposes of the agencies, the schedule of review, and the costs of such reviews.

• Boards should ask chief executive officers to share the highlights of the findings with them.

• Board members should participate along with others in periodic review of specialized accreditation practices.

Trustees should be mindful that some specialized accreditations might exhibit elements of self interest as the accrediting agency or its representatives press the institution to allocate more resources for the particular area under review.

Program Closure

In a time of declining resources, discontinuing some academic programs is an almost inevitable outcome of budget gaps and the program review practices discussed earlier. The decision whether or not to retain programs that are inconsistent with the institution's mission or strategy or that do not meet specified criteria is an integral part of the review process.

The right of institutions to engage in bona fide program closure is almost unchallenged. The AAUP, for example, accepts it as legitimate grounds for the dismissal of tenured faculty. A 1982 survey of chief academic officers in four year colleges and universities reveals that 55 percent already have established program closure policies. A number of caveats should be considered, however, before an institution develops a policy or closes a program.

First, in most cases closing a program does not save money, unless faculty are dismissed or their appointments are not renewed (Dougherty, 1981). The preamble to the University of Michigan's policy on discontinuance of academic programs specifically states that the university has *never* released tenured faculty because of program closure. Furthermore, if it should become necessary to release tenured faculty, the policy states that every effort would first be made to place them in suitable positions or to retrain them for other spots.

Second, in most cases, programs cannot be closed fast enough to be of any significance in handling short-term budget cuts or cash flow problems. Such crises demand immediate responses and program closure takes time (Melchiori, 1982, p. 22).

Third, an institutional decision to reduce the size of the faculty or engage in reductions in force (layoffs) need not be a decision to close programs. For example, when The Pennsylvania State College and University system decided to retrench in 1976 and 1980 the *preservation* of program coverage and vitality was one criterion in the selection of faculty to be terminated. (Mortimer, 1981, p. 159)

Fourth, faculty do not close programs. After an extensive review of program closure in ten universities, Dougherty concluded as follows:

> The most important thing about control and leadership as it relates to program discontinuance is that there were virtually no cases in which programs were closed as a result of faculty actions. Faculty don't close programs, for a variety of reasons. They are concerned about the moral and legal obligations to their colleagues; they fear setting off a downward spiral of decline; and they are reluctant to make a final judgment of a colleague's quality. (1981, p. 26)

Fifth, there are substantial technical, bureaucratic, and emotional barriers to overcome when considering phasing out programs. Davis and Dougherty (1978) identify the following problems:
- Lack of a data base to interpret criteria.
- Time-consuming involvement of academic officers and faculty.
- Emotionalism and resulting decreased objectivity.
- Faculty distrust.
- Ambivalence or unwillingness to make decisions.
- Political factors—many constituents try to "save their program."

In the face of these difficultites, one might ask: Why bother to close programs? Simply stated, program closure is one of many tactics to allow an institution to reallocate resources, and it is a necessary ingredient in any comprehensive strategy for improving institutional quality.

With respect to trustee involvement in program closure, three points are important. First, only the board should have the authority to close programs. Program review by state level agencies can result in demands to close programs. Trustees should anticipate such demands and make sure that reasonable arguments can be made for continuance of weaker programs when keeping them is justified. Absent such arguments, institutions should be prepared to close these programs *before* the situation degenerates into an order from the state. As a corollary to this first point, trustees should not delegate the authority to close programs to administrative or faculty bodies.

Second, a proposal to close a program must be accompanied by a plan to phase it out. This phaseout plan must be sensitive to faculty employment interests, the programmatic needs of students currently enrolled, the impact closure will have on other programs, and the reactions of influential constituencies. Trustees should recognize that once the decision to close a program has been announced, few new students are likely to enroll. In any case, a date should be set to discontinue admissions.

It is probable that many legal issues will arise if the closure results in faculty dismissals or alleged violations of students' rights. If the reason for closure is to save money, trustees must ask to see where the savings are to be realized.

Third, once trustees make the decision to close a program, they should be prepared to defend the institution and its officers from constituent pressures. Irate legislators may threaten punishment at appropriations time. Alumni of the program may threaten to withdraw financial support. Students in the program may demonstrate against the closure. But, once the decision is made, the board must be prepared to defend it, and this means every member. As John Nason states it:

> It can well be that a board will adopt policies with which some member does not agree. In such cases, the individual must accept the majority decision and defend it, if necessary, in public; or, if the issue is so momentous that the trustee cannot do this in good faith, then he or she should resign. (1982, p. 38)

Summary

There are five general questions for trustees to ask about program approval, review and closure. (The reader might want to look again at the section on general education for questions that trustees should ask in this area.)

First, who has the authority to approve, review, or close programs? Trustees should retain authority to approve or close programs. Program review will depend on institutional practices but trustees should see that the review is done.

Second, what programs are to be reviewed? Some institutions have found that a periodic cycle of reviews, such as each program every 10 years, is unnecessarily burdensome. If data bases are adequate to the task, a set of indicators can be developed which will select programs that are in need of review. For example, if enrollments fall precipitously, costs rise too quickly, or there is a significant turnover in faculty or in program leadership, a review might be in order.

The matter of defining levels of program review can be a problem for those institutions with significant graduate programs. Trustees should ask for evidence that reviews of undergraduate and graduate programs in the same department are linked and compared. In some cases the entire department would be the more appropriate unit to be reviewed.

Third, what criteria and hence what data are to govern the reviews? The data and criteria must be appropriate to making value judgments on both qualitative and quantitative grounds. Trustees must insist on knowing the relative weight given to the criteria of centrality to mission, cost, quality, and demand.

Fourth, what process is to be used? The primary purposes of a review process have been historically formative— to improve the program. When used for accreditation, certification, continuation of funding, or program approval or closure, however, the process becomes summative. In these latter cases, distrust and suspicion are more likely to occur.

Fifth, trustees must insist that the process result in operative decisions. If a program is very weak, trustees must see that it is improved or closed. If recommendations are made, they must receive serious consideration. When programs are closed they must be accompanied by a phase-out plan that is sensitive to the employment and education interests of all parties.

CHAPTER V

Academic Budgets

BARBARA E. TAYLOR

T he academic budget is a plan describing anticipated academic revenues and expenditures for a fixed period of time, usually a year. That the budget is the *plan* is the crucial point. Not even the wealthiest college or university has all the funds it can use. Resource scarcity requires institutions to make choices from among many possible expenditures. These choices form a short-term plan that should support the institution's longer-range program plans.

How can the board promote optimal use of scarce resources? This concern underlies the present chapter. Instruction, research, and academic support—the items most closely allied with the academic mission—consume approximately two-thirds of the average institution's operating budget. And most if not all of the remainder of the budget is connected indirectly with the academic mission. The ability to develop and execute the academic budget will largely determine an institution's future condition and quality.

Many trustees feel comfortable with the budget's mechanical

aspects. Corporate executives, attorneys, and business people can read a balance sheet, understand investment policies, and consider contractors' bids to provide campus services. Such skills are valuable but not sufficient. Financial stewardship of academic affairs involves obtaining answers to prior questions of institutional purpose and character. Which programs are essential? Which could be curtailed? Which programs are future students likely to find most attractive? What is the faculty's age and tenure profile? The answers to these and many other questions that might appear to have nothing to do with budgets actually form the value and information base upon which budget decisions should rest.

Academic Affairs Committee members are sometimes uneasy with this broadened view of academic budgeting, and their discomfort is compounded by two erroneous views of budgeting that enjoy currency on many campuses. The first view is that the institution should be "run like a (for-profit) corporation." In fact, colleges and universities are not profit-seeking. The "bottom line" that dictates many business budgeting decisions determines less and influences less in higher education. This is not to suggest that colleges and universities should not be *businesslike* in their management of resources, but rather to emphasize that the substantial differences between not-for-profit and for-profit organizations have consequences for budgeting.

At the other extreme rests a second erroneous view: that budgeting is somehow contrary to the lofty purposes of higher education. How, after all, can one put a price on classics? How can one choose between chemistry and German? Why should the college be concerned if a graduate course in Chaucer enrolls only two students? The problem with this thinking is that while all these activities might be "priceless" in the cultural sense, they all cost money as well. And money spent on chemistry cannot be spent on Chaucer. When choices must be made, budgeting is essential.

Influences on Academic Budgeting
A variety of distinctive organizational features complicates

academic budgeting. Here are five of the most important:

1. *The faculty of most colleges expect to be and should be involved in the budgeting process.* How to make the best use of limited funds for a given department or program should be decided by the faculty or at the very least by the administration with the benefit of faculty consultation. It would be counterproductive to devise an academic budgeting process that does not make use of faculty academic expertise.

2. *Colleges and universities typically do not know exactly what they hope to accomplish, or exactly how to accomplish it.* Lacking a tangible product, a profit motive, and a known "best way" to perform each institutional activity, institutions of higher education often experience great difficulty in choosing among possible items of expenditure. Would it be more desirable to spend scarce funds to try to increase the Graduate Record Exam scores of graduating seniors or to try to keep computer science faculty from moving to competitive institutions? Assuming the latter goal is selected, how might the funds be spent most effectively? On salary increases? New equipment? Sabbatical leaves?

3. *Total revenue and expenditure figures mean little because of restrictions on the use of many funds.* Grant and contract monies awarded to faculty members by foundations and government agencies must be spent for the specified purposes and within a designated time frame. State and federal loans and grants which subsidize student costs may not be used for other purposes. Some endowment income is restricted to particular uses. In short, a "profit and loss statement" for a given year tells the academic affairs committee little about the institution's financial condition.

4. *The operating budget, and the large percentage designated for academic purposes, can convey a deceptive sense of prosperity and flexibility.* Over the short term, 95 percent or more of the institution's expenditures are committed well in advance of the adoption of a budget. College and university budgets are normally predicated on the assumption that the institution will pay the salaries of tenured faculty members until they resign or

retire. Academic programs require certain minimal supplies and educational materials; buildings must be heated, lighted, and cleaned. Program accreditation involves the costs of institutional membership in professional associations.

If the budget is largely predetermined over the short run, it is somewhat more manipulable over a longer period. By planning ahead, the institution might be able to preclude new long-term financial commitments and increase accordingly financial flexibility in the future.

5. *Planned operating budgets are based heavily on income projections, which in turn are based largely on anticipated enrollments and government appropriations*. Private institutions are often extremely tuition-dependent; and enrollment decline of even a few students can spell disaster for a budget that appeared to be balanced. Many public colleges are also tuition-dependent, not only because tuition is an important source of operating revenues, but also because state funding formulas are often based on enrollments.

All public and many private institutions receive direct and indirect financial support from federal, state, and local governments. The timing of these funding decisions is often such that the institution's expenditures for the upcoming year are determined before revenues from government sources are. When the government fails to appropriate funds as anticipated, institutional budgets can be thrown into chaos.

Approaches to Budgeting

Budget processes in individual colleges and universities usually conform to one (or a combination) of three philosophies or styles of budgeting. The first and the least common is the *free market* approach, sometimes referred to as "each tub on its own bottom." Here units of the institution—departments, schools, or colleges—retain the income they generate and disperse it to cover their expenses. Deficits are not subsidized by some central source of funds; the unit bears the burden to maintain a balanced budget.

Thus, the department or college must appoint, retain, and remunerate faculty members and purchase other goods and services in accord with the limits and constraints of *its* resource base. Services that can be supplied only by the institution, such as libraries and central administration, are supported with assessments levied on the units.

The free market approach has obvious advantages: It encourages units to generate and conserve funds; it probably fosters a higher level of service from support agencies which must compete for business with other providers; and it relieves trustees and central managers of an obligation to select from among dozens of competing requests for funds. Fundamentally, the free market approach imbues the budgeting process at all levels with a sense of reality. Those who provide a desired and competitive product prosper while the inefficient, unpopular, or untried decline and perhaps ultimately disappear.

The free market approach, however, imposes conditions some institutions consider disadvantageous. It accentuates a departmental or territorial view at the expense of an institutional view; the whole becomes exactly the sum of its parts and no more than that. To mitigate this concern, the institution may levy a charge against all units in order to accumulate a central fund to support programs judged important but not cost-effective. Unless judiciously applied, such a limitation will destroy the principle of the free market approach.

A second possible disadvantage of the free market system is that it can minimize cooperation and foster excessive competition. Cooperative ventures and interdisciplinary programs can derive more from financial than academic considerations. Different components of the same university can pursue the same markets and the same prospective donors. An unhealthy competition can result. Moreover, the fight cannot always be fair. Hard work, excellent faculty, and entrepreneurial zeal notwithstanding, a school of education or divinity is unlikely to attract the enrollment, gifts, or research contracts that accrue to even a mediocre school of business administration or medicine. The board and president who adopt this budget scheme might confront the prospect of watching an academically superior department or school atrophy because of an inability to attract funds.

Rational approaches to budgeting, including Planning, Programming, and Budgeting Systems (PPBS) and zero-based budgeting, reflect a second budgeting philosophy. Despite differences in execution, these approaches all attempt to tie program priorities to resource allocation decisions in order to make optimal use of available funds.

As its name implies, PPBS is a three step, integrated process. First, the institution develops long-range plans. Programming decisions follow that determine the specific steps the institution will take to realize its plans. Finally, at the budgeting stage, financial allocations are made that will support program priorities. (Caruthers and Orwig, 1979)

Zero-based budgeting, like PPBS, emphasizes the link between programs and budgets. Its particular focus is on the annual rejustification of *all* expenditures. Briefly, each organizational activity for which funds are sought must be described each year in a "decision package." The package includes the activity's purposes, the likely consequences of failure to perform the activity, alternative means of fulfilling the activity's purposes, and the activity's costs and benefits. Packages are then ranked by management, and funds are allocated according to each package's priority (Caruthers and Orwig, 1979).

Rational approaches to budgeting offer one means of establishing congruence between institutional programs and expenditures. The idea that scarce resources should be used to support the institution's highest priorities is a compelling one. Yet most institutions of higher education have failed to adopt or to maintain these approaches to budgeting.

Why the lack of success? First, neither technique can be employed effectively without integrating it into the institution's social and organizational structure. Both the data and the extent of participation required to implement these approaches can be formidable. Particularly in the case of zero-based budgeting, the annual preparation and ranking of decision packages is thought by some to be impossible to do well without devoting excessive resources to the task. Second, neither approach recognizes the limits on rationality in the budget process. Colleges and universities often spend money in ways dictated by institutional history and values. These intangible yet influential qualities might be over-looked or underestimated in applying rational budget processes that emphasize the quantifiable.

Perhaps more critically, zero-based budgeting and, to a large degree, PPBS assume a flexibility in the budget that is not characteristic of colleges and universities. Continuing financial com-mitments comprise a large portion of most college and university budgets. Rejustifying expenditures for items over which the institu-tion has no short-term control strikes many as a pointless exercise.

The perceived limitations of other approaches induce many colleges and universities to rely on *incremental* budgeting, the oldest and still probably the most popular budgeting style in higher education. In incremental budgeting, most budget items are increased (or, more recently, decreased) by a comparatively modest amount from last year's level of support. In exceptional cases an item can be left unchanged or increased (or decreased) by a larger increment than other budget items. In general, the current budget is assumed to be properly distributed and in need only of minor adjustments.

The popularity of incremental budgeting should be no sur-prise. It is simple to administer, it is unlikely to cause controver-sies on campus, and it reflects the reality that most college and university expenditures are relatively fixed in the short term.

The main disadvantage of incremental budgeting arises from its presumption that, once properly distributed, the budget need not change fundamentally. This may be true over the short run, but over the longer term college and university offerings do—or should— change with societal needs and student interests. It could be that just as some rational approaches to budgeting suggest that budgets are more manipulable than they are, incrementalism implies that they are less manipulable than they can be.

The author believes that a variation of rational budgeting (described below) will best enable institutions to respond effectively to changing circumstances.

The academic affairs committee should understand the budgeting approach its college or university employs, explore the strengths and weaknesses of the approach in the academic realm, and attempt to determine whether modifications are in order. Questions that members of the Academic Affairs Committee might consider raising include:

1. What is our approach to budgeting in the academic sphere? If we use some combination of approaches, to what portions of the budget and over what periods of time is each applied?

2. Have we selected our approach to budgeting deliberately?

3. What academic goals do we expect our budgeting approach to serve?

4. Is there congruence between our academic goals and our approach to budgeting?

5. What resources are we willing to devote to the budgeting process? Do we have data, personnel, and skills commensurate with the approach we select? If not, can we obtain them?

6. Do most trustees, managers, and faculty members understand our approach to academic budgeting? Could we anticipate support for contemplated changes?

Understanding the Academic Budget

Budgets include both anticipated revenues and planned expenditures based on these revenues. While expenditures are the Academic Affairs Committee's primary budget concern, the committee should also understand the revenue side of the budget because the flow of revenues conditions academic expenditures.

Revenues

Operating revenues derive from several sources, although

the importance of any particular source varies considerably by institutional type and even by institution. The following table displays by institutional control, for all American colleges and universities, the percentage of total current fund revenue derived from each source in fiscal year 1980 (National Center for Education Statistics, 1981).

Revenue Source	All Institutions	Public Institutions	Private Institutions
Tuition	20.4	12.5	35.9
Federal, State, and Local Government Appropriations	34.4	50.8	2.1
Government Grants and Contracts	14.9	12.3	20.0
Private Gifts, Grants, and Contracts	4.8	2.5	9.3
Endowment Income	2.0	0.5	5.0
Sales and Services of Auxiliary Enterprises	20.7	19.2	23.6
Other Sources	2.8	2.2	3.9

Predictably, tuition is, on average, the most important revenue source for private colleges and universities, while government appropriations are the most important source for public institutions. When income from auxiliary services, which ordinarily is used only to offset the costs of these services, is removed from the current fund revenue totals, the importance of tuition and government appropriations is even more pronounced.

Past and predicted revenue trends provide a context for understanding the significance of particular revenue figures. Unfortunately, past income is not always an adequate predictor of future revenues. Demographics, political decisions, general economic trends, and public opinion change over time and affect institutional income. While institutions must forecast revenues in order to plan and budget, several scenarios, based on alternative sets of revenue assumptions, should be developed to compensate for the hazards of prediction.

In considering the revenue side of the proposed budget, trustees might consider asking such questions as the following:

1. What assumptions about enrollment, private giving, endowment earnings, government appropriations, and so on underlie our revenue predictions for this budget? How tentative are these assumptions? How accurate were our assumptions in the last few years?

2. How would we respond if actual revenues were X or Y percent more or less than predicted?

3. What environmental factors are likely to affect revenues five years from now? What are our revenue predictions for this period? How confident are we that these predictions are accurate? What changes in the environment would cause us to change our forecasts?

4. What actions should we be taking now to increase the likelihood that future revenues will be adequate, e.g., fund raising, new programs, investment strategies, cost savings?

Expenditures

The following table shows, by institutional control, for fiscal year 1980 the percentage of total current funds expended for various purposes by all American colleges and universities (National Center for Education Statistics, 1981).

Purpose	All Institutions	Public Institutions	Private Institutions
Instruction	32.5	35.3	27.0
Research	9.0	9.0	8.8
Public Service	3.2	4.0	1.6
Academic Support	6.8	7.4	5.7
Student Services	4.5	4.6	4.2
Institutional Support	8.9	8.3	10.0
Operation and Maintenance of Plant	8.3	8.7	7.5
Scholarships and Fellowships	3.9	2.6	6.4
Educational and General Mandatory Transfers	1.3	1.3	1.4
Auxiliary Enterprises, Hospitals, and Independent Operations	21.8	18.9	27.4

The categories of instruction, research, and academic support include all expenses directly associated with academic programs, funded research (whether with institutional or external money), and such support functions as academic administration, libraries, and academic computing facilities. These activities consumed, on average, approximately 48 percent of the total national higher education operating budget in 1980. When funds for auxiliary enterprises, hospitals, and independent operations are subtracted, they accounted for 62 percent.

The assumption that instruction, research, and academic support constitute the entire academic budget requires some qualification. One might argue that all institutional expenditures are academic, since every expenditure should support the academic mission. Otherwise the institution would presumably have no need for that particular support function. At a minimum, it seems reasonable to state that academic expenditures consume well over half the budget, exclusive of self-supporting activities, and arguably considerably more.

Academic Cost Concepts

Members of an academic affairs committee should be familiar with various cost concepts that influence the academic budget. First, colleges and universities differentiate among *direct*, *indirect*, and *full* costs. The *direct* costs of an academic program include that portion of faculty compensation attributable to the program, as well as the costs of materials and services actually consumed by the program. *Indirect* costs include maintenance and housekeeping, central administration, library, and other expenditures that support but are not used exclusively by the program. *Full* costs are the sum of direct and indirect costs.

Direct costs are relatively simple to calculate. Indirect costs are more difficult to determine because they include numerous, sometimes indeterminate, items whose costs are shared by many programs. Consequently, some administrators and faculty are tempted to count only direct costs when considering program expenditures. This approach can lead to serious underestimation of full costs as decisions are made to establish, expand, reduce, or eliminate academic programs and activities.

The Academic Affairs Committee should ensure that full costs are estimated, even if imperfectly, before the committee is asked to approve or recommend program changes with financial implications.

A college or university that decides to eliminate a program in order to save money will probably not, to its chagrin, realize savings equal to the program's full costs. The concepts of *fixed*, *variable*, and *marginal* costs explain why this is so. *Fixed* costs do not vary with the institution's level of activity. Debt on physical plant, commitments to tenured faculty (unless they are terminated), and the costs of maintaining buildings do not vary over the short run, regardless of enrollments or the extent of program offerings.

Variable costs are those that change with the institution's level of activity. Total faculty compensation, consumable supplies, and scholarship expenditures are variable costs because they normally change with enrollment and the extent of program offerings. In practice, distinguishing fixed from variable costs can be difficult. Changes in long-term financial commitments can turn a fixed cost into a variable one as, for example, when an institution replaces a tenured faculty member with a non-tenured person. Variable costs often are treated as fixed over the short run. While staff and faculty size should vary with enrollment, few institutions respond to a small enrollment decline with immediate layoffs.

Marginal costs are the additional expenditures required for each additional unit of activity. For example, if the average full cost of operating an academic program is $1,000 per student enrolled, and one additional student enrolls in the program, the expenditures associated with enrolling that particular student comprise the marginal costs. In fact, the marginal cost of one additional student is likely to be little or nothing. It may be necessary to add (or subtract) many students before full program costs are affected.

While difficult to calculate precisely, the concept of marginal costing is important as program expansion and contraction are considered. The *average* cost per unit of activity will neither be saved if the program is cut by one unit, nor spent if the program is increased by one unit. For this reason, as the Academic Affairs Committee considers proposals to expand or reduce programs, it should be concerned about anticipated marginal expenditures or savings, even if these can only be approximated.

Opportunity costs are conceptual rather than actual expenditures. These are the benefits surrendered when one purchase is made rather than another. For example, the opportunity cost of hiring a faculty member might be the reduction of travel funds for other faculty. Because we rarely know to what exact alternative use expended funds would have been put, opportunity costs are usually incalculable. As a way of thinking about proposed expenditures, however, the concept is important. When the Academic Affairs Committee is asked to recommend an academic expenditure, the justification should rest not only on the institution's ability to finance the purchase, but on the value of alternative uses to which the money could be put.

Start-up and *nonrecurring* program costs are initial or one time expenditures that often pose special problems for adminstrators, the Academic Affairs Committee, and the board. *Start-up* costs are generally associated with opening a new program. When faculty and facilities already exist to support the proposed program, start-up costs might be few or none. Conversely, opening a new program for which faculty, facilities, equipment, and educational materials are required can be most expensive. Supporters of a new program usually tend to minimize start-up expenditures and to maximize estimates of the program's payoff to the institution. The Academic Affairs Committee should beware of proposed programs that, for example, promise throngs of new students with little or no additional cost to the institution.

Proposals for new programs should routinely include detailed estimates of start-up costs. If these costs are to be spread over several years, multi-year estimates should be provided. If possible, cost estimates should be prepared or verified by a disinterested party such as an office of budgeting or institutional research. The start-up costs incurred by other institutions that opened comparable programs might be another source of useful guidance. In any event, the Academic Affairs Committee should not approve new programs without a clear understanding of the programs' likely costs and benefits.

Nonrecurring program costs are special expenditures that are repeated infrequently if ever. These are often capital purchases—new buildings, major facility renovations, or equipment, for example.

Such expenditures pose two often difficult problems. First,

in requiring exceptional financial commitments, nonrecurring expenses could disrupt incremental budgeting practices. Second, and more important, these expenditures are usually sizable. The cost of a new building, a major laboratory, or a large computer could easily deplete the institution's operating and capital reserves, and frequently can be financed only with borrowed funds, a capital fund campaign, or a special government appropriation. For these reasons, nonrecurring expenditures should be anticipated and planned as far in advance as possible.

The Academic Affairs Committee and the governing board should encourage the institution to develop a multi-year plan for nonrecurring academic expenditures.

Productivity Measures

An Academic Affairs Committee that knows a program's cost but not its yield will have difficulty ensuring optimal use of academic funds. Various productivity measures can help an institution gauge the relationship between expenditure and yield. Many colleges and universities routinely produce reports by department or program of costs per student credit hour, costs per faculty member, and changes in these costs over time. Such data should be interpreted warily, since some programs are inherently more expensive than others and because the institution might consciously decide to allocate more resources to programs deemed particularly distinctive or on the threshold of excellence.

An especially useful device for understanding departmental and program productivity is the Induced Course Load Matrix (or ICLM) developed by the National Center for Higher Education Management Systems. The ICLM shows student credit hour enrollment by department and by student major.

The ICLM may show, for example, that biology majors accounted for 50 percent of the institution's enrollment in biology courses, 2 percent in art courses, and 10 percent in English courses. The ICLM demonstrates graphically the crucial difference between a department's production of majors and of credit hours. Relatively few students might major in physics, but that department could generate many credit hours as students from other majors enroll in physics courses.

In addition to informing resource allocation decisions, the ICLM can be useful in personnel planning. A department that primarily serves upper division and graduate students might need a different mix of faculty from the department whose enrollment is mostly nonmajor freshmen.

Quantitative productivity is readily measured. Qualitative results are more difficult but not impossible to assess. Program quality assessments of the sort recently undertaken by the Conference Board of Associated Research Councils can provide the Academic Affairs Committee at a research university with an idea of the relative standing of their institution's programs. External reviewers can be brought to the campus to assess program and faculty quality. Changes in student achievement between entrance and graduation can be studied, and faculty performance can be reviewed by students and by departmental colleagues.

Some of the questions the Academic Affairs Committee might wish to ask about academic expenditures include the following:

1. Do we consider full costs in planning program establishment, expansion, reduction, and elimination? What indirect expenses are assigned to programs?

2. Can we estimate marginal expenditures and savings associated with changes in institutional programs and activities?

3. Are we satisfied that academic expenditures proposed are not only financially feasible, but also represent optimal use of available funds? To what other purposes might the funds be applied?

4. What are our program cost predictions for the next several years? How confident are we that these predictions are accurate?

5. If future program costs are higher or lower than anticipated by X or Y percent, how will we respond?

6. Do we monitor the costs per credit for departments and programs? What are the trends in these costs? How can we plan, if necessary, to realign program costs?

7. Do we have a multi-year plan for financing nonrecurring expenditures?

8. Do we have a reliable means of estimating start-up costs for new programs? Do we consider these costs before instituting new programs?

9. How do we measure productivity? How do we assess the relationships between quality and cost?

Interrelationships Among Revenues and Expenditures

The Academic Affairs Committee and the board more generally must understand the complex interplay between revenues and expenditures in order to comprehend the effects of changes in individual revenue and expenditure categories. One useful tool for this purpose is the "source-use concept," developed by the National Center for Higher Education Management Systems (NCHEMS) (Allen and Collier, 1980). The concept is based on the type of matrix shown below.

SOURCE							
USE	Institutional		Government	Private	Departmental	Other	Total
Faculty Compensation	$ Amount	%					
Other Compensations							
Supplies and Services							
Equipment							
Other							
Total							

The matrix can be expanded to reflect more detailed revenue and expenditure data, particularly the data categories included in the institution's auditable financial statements. The matrix reveals current financial circumstances as well as possible areas of need or weakness.

For example, a matrix showing faculty compensation largely funded by grant and contract revenue should raise questions about the status of the faculty in question. Are they temporary employees compensated with temporary money? Or will the institution be obligated to continue paying them once the "soft" money is depleted? If private gifts are shown to be directed primarily toward plant maintenance or scholarships, should the institution attempt to persuade future donors to support other projects? And, furthermore, what will happen to the institution's finances if gift giving declines?

While the source-use matrix is not a substitute for more detailed financial statements, it does offer useful, readily understood information to trustees.

Financial planning models offer a second means of understanding the complex relationship between revenues and expenditures. The best known of these is EFPM (EDUCOM Financial Planning Model), an interactive, computer-based system (Bloomfield and Updegrove, 1982). EFPM allows users to specify assumptions about various revenue and expenditure levels, and to determine which combinations are actually feasible. For example, the college that wishes to raise faculty salaries by seven percent can use EFPM to explore possible combinations of revenue changes to fund the increase.

Financial planning models allow their users to test a range of possible budget alternatives quickly and easily. While such models cannot make decisions, they are valuable for informing decision makers. The Academic Affairs Committee might wish to ask institutional personnel such questions as the following:

1. Do we use the source-use matrix, EFPM, or a comparable

device to understand relationships between our revenues and expenditures?

2. What have been the trends in these relationships over time?

3. Do the data suggest financial problems we should be addressing in the academic area?

BUDGET MAKING

Phases of the Academic Budget Process

The process by which the budget is created varies according to the budgeting approach the college or university adopts. The author recommends a process described by Caruthers and Orwig (1979) that is closely related to rational budgeting. Because rationality implies that budgeting and planning will be allied, this budgeting process begins with a planning phase. Here, major institutional decisions are made with concern for creating and maintaining consonance between the college or university and its environment. Such "strategic" planning is an ongoing process.

Trustees normally do not develop institutional strategy, but rather specify that managers do so in collaboration with the faculty. Nevertheless, the board's role as prodder and then as final arbiter of strategic decisions is a central one.

The second phase of the budgeting process, program planning, involves identifying program priorities that are consistent with the institution's strategic plans, and estimating the associated costs and revenues. While institutional personnel should be expected to recommend program priorities, trustees should consider these recommendations and either approve them or suggest reconsideration. Similarly, revenue and expenditure estimates are made by administrative staff, but trustees might inquire about the assumptions on which these estimates are based.

In the third phase of the budgeting process, documents are prepared that serve as the institution's formal budget proposal—

whether presented to the governing board, the legislature, or a state education agency. Budget documents should reflect the priorities identified during the strategic and program-planning phases. While preliminary budget documents may be prepared at the institution's department and school levels, the final proposal incorporating these into one request is generally the work of senior management.

Participants

Many constituent groups are properly interested in helping to establish expenditure priorities. The budgeting approach the institution adopts largely influences the composition of the principal participants in the process. Under a free market arrangement, most budgeting decisions are made at the department, school, or academic college level and therefore involve faculty, department chairpersons, and academic deans. A rational approach that ties budgets to overall institutional priorities will probably require more extensive involvement by senior managers, typically with the advice of faculty, chairpersons, and deans. A purely incremental approach, on the other hand, could be implemented by staff members in the budget office instructed to add (or subtract) some percentage from each item in the previous year's budget.

While the budgeting approach dictates who *must* be involved in the process, the matter of who else might be involved is open. A budget process that relies on planning, but does not include faculty and staff in the planning process, is likely to be ineffective. Advisory and study committees that include a broad range of constituent representatives can provide useful guidance to budget makers.

Some institutions employ a hearing process in which departments and other units present their budget requests to such a committee. The hearing can provide a forum for discussing departmental needs, priorities, and contributions, supplementing the information contained in budget documents.

The Academic Affairs Committee shares with the Finance Committee a keen interest in the academic budget. That common concern raises questions about how budget authority can best be allocated. The Finance Committee should assume responsibility for approving the revenue estimates on which the academic budget is based. Moreover, it should work with the Academic Affairs Committee and management to determine both the total amount to be allotted to academic expenditures and the general priorities to be followed in allocating these funds. When the Academic Affairs Committee is prepared to recommend an academic budget, it might make its presentation first to the Finance Committee, and then to the full board.

BUDGETING ISSUES

The Context of Budget Decisions

The Academic Affairs Committee should consider whether planned academic expenditures take into account anticipated changes in the college's environment. Academic budget requests should routinely include statements and supporting data about the relationship of the request to external factors affecting the institution. The committee might, therefore, ask such questions as:

1. How have program enrollments shifted over the past several years? Have resources been reallocated accordingly? Are we developing plans for future resource reallocation?

2. What trends are evident in our receipt of government grants and appropriations? Do these reflect support for our programs by the legislature and funding agencies?

3. What effects are social and technological changes likely to have? How responsive can and should our programs be to these changes?

4. How is the pool of potential students changing? Are our academic offerings and services pertinent to these students?

5. What strategies are our competitors using? Where do we enjoy a competitive advantage?

Financial Condition

Because budgets are central to the operation of colleges and universities, we often look to budgetary data for evidence of the institution's financial condition. Most people assume that a balanced budget equals good financial condition. In fact, budgets may be balanced by deferring maintenance, paying faculty poorly, or enrolling students who are academically underprepared. Conversely, while anticipating new revenues from a major fund-raising drive, an institution might decide to operate at a deficit for a few years in order to build a promising program or retain an excellent faculty.

In short, financial data require interpretation in order to be useful as evidence of true financial condition.

Financial ratios are particularly helpful for enhancing data interpretability. The ratio of instructional expenditures to students enrolled or credit hours generated in a given year can be a useful indicator of financial condition. First, it can be compared to the same ratio from earlier years, and used to show trends in instructional costs. Second, it can be compared to instructional expenditures per student in peer institutions and used to show variations in interinstitutional costs.

In either case, the Academic Affairs Committee might ask questions about what observed trends or differences mean. What factors account for changes in instructional costs? If costs have risen, where have the additional funds expended come from? Why are our instructional costs higher (or lower) than those of our peer institutions? Are cost variations among our programs justifiable?

Hundreds of financial ratios can be calculated from readily available institutional financial statements. Peer institutions are often enthusiastic about sharing data, since most colleges and universities are curious about where they stand vis-à-vis peers. Some accounting firms, notably Peat, Marwick, Mitchell and Company, (Minter, Nelson, and Robinson, 1980) provide financial ratios, trend information and peer group comparisons for their college and university clients. While ratios are usually suggestive rather than conclusive, they can be valuable tools for monitoring financial condition.

Conclusion

The science of economics is based on the simple observation that choices must be made from among competing possible uses of scarce resources. This is the fundamental fact of college and university budgets as well. A single dollar cannot be spent twice.

The sometimes formidable mechanics of the budget process should not be allowed to obscure the fact that budgets pay for institutional priorities, whether those priorities are selected explicitly or thrust by circumstance on the institution. When contemplating the academic budget, the Academic Affairs Committee is wise to consider—and to encourage administrators and faculty members, as well as the board, to consider—the issue of resource scarcity and its relationship to institutional priorities.

"Can we afford it?" is not the only possible question. An equally crucial and a far more difficult question can be asked: "Is this the best possible use of these resources?"

Self-Study Questionnaire

SUGGESTIONS TO USERS

Academic Affairs and Trustee Overseeing

Overseeing academic affairs is an intellectually demanding and often delicate task for trustees, particularly those assigned to the Academic Affairs Committee. Embedded in the issues that come before the committee are values that define the character of the institution. The committee's judgments, therefore, often have both immediate and long-range effects on the professional lives of faculty and the educational programs of students.

As "lay" board members, many trustees have had limited exposure to academic plans and budgets, educational programs, and faculty personnel policies. Furthermore, given the complexity of higher education and the difficulty of distinguishing between policy making and administrative responsibilities, trustees on the Academic Affairs Committee can find it difficult to define an appropriate role which both capitalizes on their unique perspective on the institution and which acknowledges and encourages the expertise and involvement of the faculty.

Method

This self-study survey has been designed to assist members of academic affairs committees to understand more fully the wide range of issues associated with overseeing academic programs and faculty personnel policies. Since committee involvement varies significantly from institution to institution, the survey is intended primarily to facilitate discussion and stimulate thought. It is not intended to suggest or prescribe an ideal standard of performance.

At minimum, the self-study format provides an opportunity for trustees to review a number of academic issues and, in light of the distinctive character of their own institution, to evaluate the appropriate policy role of their committee in the areas of academic programs, faculty personnel, finance, academic planning, information needs, and self assessment. Responses to key questions in each of these areas should produce a composite description of the quality, nature, and effectiveness of the committee's performance.

Although the self-study survey is addressed primarily to members of the Academic Affairs Committee, the issues are germane regardless of a board's committee structure. The instrument should, therefore, be equally useful to trustees whether or not their boards employ a formal committee structure.

Planning a Self-Study Survey

1. Before undertaking the survey, the committee should agree on the purposes and usefulness of a self-study designed to offer insight into the members' views about the committee's present practices.

2. The questionnaire should be provided to each committee member. If necessary it can be mailed, preferably with a cover letter from the committee chairperson, to urge respondents to provide supplementary comments and to suggest changes for improvement. (A deadline for the return of the form should be specified.)

3. Consideration should be given to whether responses should be anonymous. In either case, a stamped, self-addressed return envelope should accompany each questionnaire.

4. A member of the institution's staff should be assigned to prepare and distribute the materials, compile responses, including a verbatim listing of all discursive responses, and to administer other details as required.

Planning the Discussion of Survey Results

The survey can be used to facilitate an hour's discussion, a series of discussions, or a mini-retreat. Whichever approach is selected, several additional points might also be helpful in planning post-survey activities:

1. A complete summary of the survey responses should be mailed to all participants in advance of a follow-up post-survey discussion.

2. Particular attention should be given to responses where there is a significant divergence of opinion.

3. If during discussion the committee determines that changes should be made, these should be compiled in writing and distributed so that all committee members, as well as institutional staff, have a record of them.

4. It might be appropriate to distribute the proposed changes to the full board for review and discussion; at the least, a report of the results of the self-study should be made to the full board.

COMMITTEE ROLE I:
OVERSEEING ACADEMIC PROGRAM POLICIES

1. Does your institution have a statement of mission and purpose?

_____Yes _____No _____Don't know or can't judge

   Is it clear?

_____Yes _____No _____Don't know or can't judge

2. If so, does the committee review periodically the adequacy of this statement?

_____Yes _____No _____Don't know or can't judge

3. Does the committee refer to the mission statement in its decision making?

_____Yes _____Usually _____Rarely _____No
_____Don't know or can't judge

4. How would you describe the committee's involvement in academic program policies with respect to:

	Recommends Policy or Action to the Full Board	Reviews and/or Sometimes Modifies Policy or Action	Not Involved
Establishing new academic programs/schools	_____	_____	_____
Significantly expanding academic programs/schools	_____	_____	_____
Significantly reducing academic programs/schools	_____	_____	_____
Terminating academic programs/schools	_____	_____	_____
Evaluating the quality of academic programs/schools	_____	_____	_____
Setting the requirements for degrees	_____	_____	_____
Establishing admissions standards	_____	_____	_____

5. Does the committee have access to the views of faculty leaders on major academic program issues?

_____Yes _____No _____Don't know or can't judge

6. Overall, the committee's *involvement* in academic program policies is:

_____Too much _____About right _____Too little
_____Don't know or can't judge

Comments:

COMMITTEE ROLE II:
OVERSEEING FACULTY PERSONNEL POLICIES

1. Does the committee review periodically the policies governing faculty advancement (i.e., promotions in rank and awards of tenure)?

_____Yes _____No _____Don't know or can't judge

2. Are these policies effective in providing due process?

_____Yes _____No _____Don't know or can't judge

3. Are these policies effective in enhancing the academic quality of the institution?

_____Yes _____No _____Don't know or can't judge

4. How would you describe the committee's involvement in faculty personnel policies with respect to:

	Recommends Policy or Action to the Full Board	Reviews and/or Sometimes Modifies Policy or Action	Not Involved
Promotions in rank	_____	_____	_____
Awarding of tenure	_____	_____	_____
Faculty evaluation	_____	_____	_____
Sabbatical leave	_____	_____	_____
Affirmative action	_____	_____	_____
Faculty development/retraining	_____	_____	_____
Faculty workload	_____	_____	_____
Faculty retirement	_____	_____	_____
Reduction in force	_____	_____	_____

5. Does the committee have access to the views of faculty leaders on major academic personnel issues?

_____Yes _____No _____Don't know or can't judge

6. Overall, the committee's *involvement* in faculty personnel policies is:

_____Too much   _____About right   _____Too little
_____Don't know or can't judge

Comments:

COMMITTEE ROLE III:
OVERSEEING ACADEMIC BUDGETING

1. How would you describe the committee's involvement in academic budgeting with respect to:

	Recommends Policy or Action to the Full Board	Reviews and/or Sometimes Modifies Policy or Action	Not Involved
Establishing the annual budget in support of academic activities	_____	_____	_____
Establishing guidelines for faculty salaries, including annual adjustments	_____	_____	_____
Ensuring that capital expenditures support the program priorities	_____	_____	_____
Evaluating income-expense data on academic programs	_____	_____	_____
Providing a benefit program for faculty, including retirement benefits	_____	_____	_____
Developing a financial exigency policy	_____	_____	_____

2. Does the committee have access to the views of faculty leaders on major academic budget issues?

_____Yes   _____No   _____Don't know or can't judge

3. Overall, the committee's *involvement* in academic budgeting is

_____Too much   _____About right   _____Too little
_____Don't know or can't judge

Comments:

COMMITTEE ROLE IV:
OVERSEEING ACADEMIC PLANNING

1. Has the board approved a comprehensive long-range plan within the past five years?

_____Yes _____No _____Don't know or can't judge

2. If so, does it adequately cover both academic program and personnel policy considerations?

_____Yes _____No _____Don't know or can't judge

3. Has the faculty had a major role in the development of this plan?

_____Yes _____No _____Don't know or can't judge

4. How would you describe the committee's *involvement* in the development of this long-range plan?

_____Too much _____About right _____Too little
_____Don't know or can't judge

Comments:

COMMITTEE ROLE V:
MEETING THE COMMITTEE'S NEED
FOR INFORMATION

1. Who determines the amount and extent of data which members of the Academic Affairs Committee receive?

_____ the committee determines   _____ the administration decides

_____ a combination of both   _____ don't know or can't judge

2. In your work as a member of the Academic Affairs Committee, which of the following people and resources have been most helpful to you? (Check as many as apply.)

_____ other trustees   _____ other faculty seen informally on
                                                  or off campus

_____ chief executive officer   _____ students assigned to the committee

_____ chief academic officer   _____ other students seen informally on
                                                  or off campus

_____ deans   _____ student newspaper

_____ other administrators   _____ institutional publication

_____ alumni/ae   _____ area newspaper

_____ legislators/   _____ *Chronicle of Higher Education*
         legislative staff

_____ faculty assigned to   _____ *AGB Reports, AGB Notes,* AGB
         the committee   conference or other AGB materials

_____ other _____

_____ other _____

3. What types of data and information have been provided to you as a committee member within the past year or two, in oral or in written form, which have been particularly valuable? (Please check as many as apply.)

_____ Regional accrediting   _____ Demographic trends and projec-
         reports (or précis)   tions of vocational opportunities

_____ Specialized accrediting   _____ Trendline data on students, e.g.
         reports (or précis),   credit hours by department,
         e.g. American Chemical   vocational surveys of recent
         Society   alumni/ae

_____Faculty self-studies
of departments or
programs

_____Critiques of the strengths
and weaknesses of the
overall academic program

_____A multi-year academic plan
which links academic
priorities to resource allocation

_____Trendline data on faculty, e.g.
percent tenured, age cohorts,
projected retirements, etc.

_____Trendline data on affirmative
action as it affects students,
faculty, and curriculum

_____Trendline data on sources of
revenue and expenditures in the
academic budget

_____Other: _____

_____

_____

4. On the basis of the information you receive from these sources, do you feel prepared to make the judgments required of you as a committee member?

_____Yes   _____Usually   _____Rarely   _____No
_____Don't know or can't judge

Comments:

COMMITTEE ROLE VI:
ASSESSING EFFECTIVENESS PERIODICALLY

1. Does the committee study adequately major alternative policy options before making a recommendation to the board?
_____Yes _____Usually _____Rarely _____No
_____Don't know or can't judge

2. Are the committee's recommendations given adequate consideration by the full board?
_____Yes _____Usually _____Rarely _____No
_____Don't know or can't judge

3. How would you describe the adequacy of opportunities for faculty leaders to be heard on major issues before the committee?
_____Very good/excellent _____Adequate _____Poor
_____Don't know or can't judge

4. How would you assess the adequacy of staffing for the committee, especially with regard to preparation of agendas and other materials in advance of the meeting, including follow up?
_____Very good/excellent _____Adequate _____Poor
_____Don't know or can't judge

5. Overall, how would you describe your committee's overseeing of academic affairs?
_____Too involved_____Adequate_____Not involved enough
_____Don't know or can't judge

6. What single change could the Academic Affairs Committee make *now* to increase its effectiveness?

_____

_____

7. What single change could the committee make *over the long term* to increase its effectiveness?

_____

_____

Comments:

Highlights of the National Survey

One major component of AGB's project on the role of trustees in academic affairs was a national survey of 549 college and university trustees and presidents. This survey was summarized and analyzed by Barbara E. Taylor. The survey concerned 1) trustee involvement in academic affairs, 2) the perceived importance of various academic issues, and 3) trustees' sources of information and channels of communication in the academic sphere.

The survey results, as well as the methodology, are discussed in detail in *Trustee Responsibility for Academic Affairs: Results of a National Survey*, available from AGB. The purpose of this appendix is to highlight and comment briefly on the major findings of the survey.

The table on page 112 presents the survey questions and reports results for all respondents and for public and private respondents separately.

PART I

Trustee Involvement in Academic Affairs

Which academic issues have arisen most frequently since 1977 at the colleges and universities surveyed?

• Evaluating the performance of the president and academic administrators (72.8%)

• Establishing new programs (70.9%)

• Appointing the president and academic administrators (70.4%)

• Establishing the annual academic budget (68.4%)

• Establishing long-range plans for academic programs (67.0%)

• Establishing faculty compensation policies (64.1%)

• Revising the institution's mission (62.7%)

Which academic issues have arisen least frequently in this period?

• Laying off tenured faculty because of financial exigency (20.4%)

• Laying off nontenured faculty because of financial exigency (23.6%)

• Declaring financial exigency (27.2%)

• Establishing guidelines for determining financial exigency (40.2%)

Comments

The academic issues that have arisen most frequently in recent years are those that presidents and trustees probably consider most essential to effective institutional functioning—appointing and evaluating the president and academic administrators, establishing programs and long-range plans, and revising the institution's mission. There are no surprises here. Those matters that have arisen with less frequency are more interesting. All concern financial exigency, which suggests that relatively few institutions have faced exigency or feel threatened enough to consider establishing guidelines and policies to govern such circumstances.

Which academic issues have arisen appreciably more often at public than at independent institutions?
- Initial appointment of faculty to nontenure-track appointments (60.2% of public institutions versus 51.8% of private institutions)
- Establishing affirmative action policies, goals, and timetables (61.6% versus 46.5%)
- Reducing existing programs (61.4% versus 52.4%)
- Discontinuing existing programs (57.6% versus 43.2%)
- Establishing academic program requirements (50.9% versus 42.4%)

Which academic issues have arisen appreciably more often at independent than at public institutions?
- Revising the institution's mission (67.2% of private institutions versus 59% of public institutions)
- Establishing faculty retirement policies (70.8% versus 46.1%)
- Establishing faculty promotion policies (51.7% versus 42.6%)
- Establishing faculty tenure policies (59.7% versus 43.5%)
- Establishing faculty compensation policies (69.1% versus 60.2%)
- Evaluating the performance of the president and academic administrators (77.9% versus 68.8%)
- Appointing the president and academic administrators (78.2% versus 64.1%)

Comments

It is the public sector rather than the supposedly more financially vulnerable independent sector that has dealt most frequently with program reduction and discontinuance. Independent institutions have reconsidered their mission more frequently than public colleges and universities, and they have been more engaged in establishing various faculty personnel policies. These data suggest that when confronted with financial difficulties the public sector tends to respond with program reductions while the independent sector turns to mission changes and money-saving modifications in personnel policies.

On which academic issues do boards tend to assume more active roles? (Listed in descending order, from most active to least active.)
- Appointing the president and academic administrators
- Revising the institution's mission
- Evaluating the performance of the president and academic administrators
- Declaring financial exigency
- Laying off tenured faculty because of financial exigency
- Establishing the annual academic budget
- Establishing guidelines for determining financial exigency
- Establishing faculty retirement policies
- Establishing faculty compensation policies
- Establishing faculty sabbatical leave policies
- Establishing new programs

On which academic issues do boards tend to assume less active roles? (Listed in ascending order, from least active to most active.)
- Evaluating the performance of individual faculty members
- Establishing faculty workloads
- Approving individual faculty salaries
- Renewing individual faculty contracts
- Making initial appointments of faculty to nontenure-track positions
- Establishing faculty evaluation procedures
- Establishing academic program requirements

Comments

Board involvement with the academic issues included in the survey is largely consistent with prevailing advice about proper board participation. Such activities as appointing and evaluating the president; revising the institution's mission; and establishing the academic budget, academic programs, and faculty personnel policies are typically cited as primary board functions. In contrast, boards are considerably less active in implementing faculty personnel policies or in establishing academic program requirements, areas over which trustees are normally advised to exercise less control.

PART II

Perceived Importance of Various Academic Issues

What do respondents judge to be the most important academic issues now facing their institutions? (Listed in descending order of importance.)

- Reviewing the strengths and weaknesses of current academic programs
- Determining, reviewing, and approving new academic programs
- Establishing a planning and budgeting process that leads to rational allocation of academic resources
- Determining which programs to reduce, eliminate, or consolidate
- Establishing faculty development programs in order to provide faculty with opportunities for professional growth

What do respondents judge to be the least important academic issues now facing their institutions? (Listed in ascending order of importance.)

- Changing admission standards in order to alter the size or composition of the student body
- Establishing affirmative action policies, goals, and

timetables in order to hire and retain more female and minority faculty members

  • Developing policies to govern the layoffs of full-time faculty for reasons of financial exigency

  • Altering general education requirements to reflect shifts in thinking about students' educational needs and interests

  • Establishing faculty development programs in order to encourage faculty to retrain and shift to fields with greater student demand

Comments

The issues that respondents judge to be relatively more important to their institutions are not particularly surprising. The fact that, in a time of demographic and economic decline, respondents judge the approval of new programs more important than the reduction or closure of existing ones is an unexpected finding, buttressed by the respondents' views of the least important academic issues. Few respondents (11.3%) consider changing admission standards to alter the size or composition of the student body "very important." Similarly, respondents judge relatively less important the establishment of faculty layoff policies for use in financial emergencies and the creation of faculty development programs to encourage retraining for teaching in high demand fields.

Apparently most respondents are not anticipating severe financial emergencies that would interrupt "business as usual." If survey respondents are aware of these hazards, they apparently believe their institutions will be spared.

PART III

Sources of Information and Channels of Communication

What do respondents believe are the board's most important sources of information on academic matters?

- The president
- Academic administrators
- Faculty government

What do respondents list as the board's most *common* means of learning faculty sentiment on academic matters?

- Academic administrators' reports of faculty viewpoints
- Contact with representatives or committees of faculty government

What do respondents list as the board's most *informative* means of learning faculty sentiment on academic matters?

- Academic administrators' reports of faculty viewpoints
- Contact with representatives or committees of faculty government

Comments

It is not surprising that trustees find administrators both important and informative sources of information on faculty opinion and on other academic matters. Boards typically have more contact with administrators than with faculty, and tend to trust the presidents they appoint.

Summary

The results of the survey simultaneously provoke optimism and concern about trustee involvement in academic affairs. Findings suggest that boards and institutional personnel give attention to many crucial academic matters, and that boards are generally more active in approving policy than in implementing it. The issues respondents identified as "very important" are among those that most experts agree are critical. Trustees apparently communicate with and trust the administrators they appoint. In contrast, most respondents do not appear to be especially concerned about the prospect of demographic and economic pressure on their institutions. Trustees and administrators would be well advised to ask themselves if their view of the future is a realistic one.

Survey Questions and Responses by Institutional Control

PART I

We are interested in learning about the involvement of your governing board in making various institutional decisions. Please indicate the type of involvement your board has had in the past five years with each of the issues listed. If the issue has not arisen in the past five years, please circle the response that would best characterize the board's behavior if the issue were to arise in the future.

Possible Responses

1—This issue would not come to the board at all.

2—The board receives information about this issue but takes no action on it.

3—The board directs the administration to take action on this issue after advice and consultation with the board.

4—The board makes the decision about this issue, although it might seek the opinions of others before doing so.

5—Do not know.

ISSUE	INSTITUTION GROUP	HAS ARISEN SINCE 1977 AT THIS % OF INSTITUTIONS	RESPONSE				
			1	2	3	4	5
Revising the	all	62.7	0.9	2.1	35.0	61.3	0.6
institution's	public	59.0	1.6	2.4	40.2	54.7	1.1
mission	private	67.2	0.0	1.9	28.5	69.6	0.0
Initial appointment							
of faculty to	all	56.3	23.5	17.8	30.6	26.7	1.4
tenure-track	public	57.6	12.9	13.9	37.6	33.3	2.2
positions	private	54.7	36.1	22.5	22.3	18.9	0.3

ISSUE	INSTITUTION GROUP	HAS ARISEN SINCE 1977 AT THIS % OF INSTITUTIONS	RESPONSE				
			1	2	3	4	5
Initial appointment of faculty to nontenure-track appointments	all	56.4	30.0	23.2	27.2	18.9	0.7
	public	60.2	12.8	17.9	36.9	30.9	1.4
	private	5.8	50.9	29.5	15.3	4.3	0.0
Renewing individual faculty contracts	all	59.0	40.2	19.4	24.4	15.3	0.8
	public	61.4	24.0	16.5	34.2	24.5	0.8
	private	55.9	60.2	23.1	12.1	3.8	0.8
Denying reappointment to faculty for other than financial reasons	all	54.5	22.5	23.2	29.4	23.3	1.7
	public	55.4	14.2	13.1	35.6	34.7	2.4
	private	53.3	32.7	35.7	21.6	9.3	0.7
Establishing faculty retirement policies	all	57.0	8.9	5.4	35.2	49.8	0.7
	public	46.1	12.1	4.8	29.2	52.7	1.2
	private	70.8	5.0	6.0	42.7	46.3	0.0
Establishing faculty evaluation procedures	all	52.6	20.2	32.0	37.5	9.5	0.8
	public	50.4	19.3	28.9	39.5	10.9	1.3
	private	55.4	21.4	35.8	34.9	7.7	0.2
Evaluating the performance of individual faculty members	all	46.7	63.2	24.4	10.9	0.8	0.6
	public	46.1	57.8	24.1	15.5	1.5	1.1
	private	47.3	69.9	24.8	5.3	0.0	0.0
Establishing faculty promotion policies	all	46.6	14.7	17.3	38.7	27.5	1.9
	public	42.6	15.5	12.4	39.6	29.3	3.2
	private	51.7	13.7	23.3	37.5	25.3	0.3
Establishing faculty tenure policies	all	50.7	11.9	6.0	38.1	42.2	1.8
	public	43.5	18.2	4.4	30.7	43.5	3.2
	private	59.7	4.5	7.8	46.7	40.7	0.3
Establishing faculty compensation policies	all	64.1	5.6	6.9	39.9	46.7	0.9
	public	60.2	7.5	5.4	33.8	52.1	1.1
	private	69.1	3.2	8.8	47.4	39.9	0.8
Approving individual faculty salaries	all	52.6	44.1	16.2	22.8	16.2	0.7
	public	54.8	24.1	16.5	31.9	26.7	0.9
	private	49.9	68.7	15.9	11.7	3.3	0.4
Establishing faculty sabbatical leave policies	all	48.3	7.4	8.1	40.1	42.0	2.4
	public	48.5	7.0	6.4	35.9	48.6	2.2
	private	48.0	7.9	10.4	45.6	33.5	2.6
Approving faculty sabbatical leaves	all	50.0	22.3	13.4	30.3	31.7	2.3
	public	52.5	12.9	6.8	34.4	42.9	2.0
	private	46.8	34.1	21.5	23.9	17.8	2.7

ISSUE	INSTITUTION GROUP	HAS ARISEN SINCE 1977 AT THIS % OF INSTITUTIONS	RESPONSE				
			1	2	3	4	5
Establishing faculty workloads	all	42.3	43.0	21.6	24.8	9.2	1.4
	public	41.4	33.1	22.1	29.3	13.6	1.9
	private	43.4	54.9	21.1	19.4	4.0	0.7
Establishing affirmative action policies, goals, and timetables	all	54.9	7.6	12.2	47.4	31.3	1.5
	public	61.6	3.8	13.1	43.9	37.7	1.2
	private	46.5	12.3	10.9	51.8	23.1	1.9
Evaluating the performance of the president and academic administrators	all	72.8	2.5	5.0	24.7	66.0	1.9
	public	68.8	2.9	3.8	27.5	62.6	3.1
	private	77.9	1.9	6.5	20.9	70.4	0.2
Appointing the president and academic administrators	all	70.4	1.3	1.0	19.0	78.3	0.4
	public	64.1	1.2	0.5	18.7	79.1	0.6
	private	78.2	1.4	1.7	19.5	77.3	0.2
Establishing long-range plans for academic administrators	all	67.0	1.7	14.2	64.1	19.5	0.5
	public	66.2	1.2	11.2	66.4	20.5	0.6
	private	68.0	2.5	17.9	61.2	18.1	0.3
Establishing new programs	all	70.9	1.9	13.3	49.3	35.5	0.0
	public	71.0	1.8	6.7	51.0	40.3	0.0
	private	70.8	2.0	21.7	47.1	29.2	0.0
Expanding existing programs	all	64.5	6.5	30.4	47.8	15.2	0.0
	public	65.1	5.8	21.9	54.1	18.1	0.0
	private	63.9	7.5	41.2	39.8	11.5	0.0
Reducing existing programs	all	57.4	6.2	24.1	53.9	15.1	0.7
	public	61.4	5.2	19.9	56.3	18.1	0.6
	private	52.4	7.5	29.5	50.8	11.3	0.9
Requiring that academic programs be evaluated	all	47.2	7.8	22.7	48.4	18.4	2.7
	public	52.0	6.5	22.3	45.5	23.8	1.9
	private	40.9	9.4	23.3	52.2	11.4	3.7
Discontinuing existing programs	all	51.2	3.3	15.7	48.2	30.9	2.0
	public	57.6	2.1	9.1	49.4	36.4	3.0
	private	43.2	4.8	23.9	46.6	24.1	0.7
Establishing academic program requirements	all	47.1	22.5	31.8	34.1	10.6	1.1
	public	50.9	17.1	31.5	36.6	15.1	0.6
	private	42.4	29.3	32.0	32.2	4.9	1.6
Establishing admissions criteria and policies	all	48.4	17.5	26.7	37.6	17.4	0.9
	public	47.9	15.7	17.5	39.5	26.2	1.1
	private	49.0	19.7	38.0	35.2	6.4	0.7

ISSUE	INSTITUTION GROUP	HAS ARISEN SINCE 1977 AT THIS % OF INSTITUTIONS	RESPONSE				
			1	2	3	4	5
Establishing the	all	68.4	2.9	2.3	42.5	51.9	0.4
annual academic	public	69.1	3.1	2.2	45.4	48.6	0.6
budget	private	67.6	2.5	2.5	38.7	56.1	0.2
Establishing guidelines	all	40.2	2.5	3.8	45.2	44.4	4.0
for determining	public	43.3	3.7	5.6	46.7	39.7	4.3
financial exigency	private	36.2	1.1	1.7	43.4	50.3	3.6
Declaring	all	27.1	2.3	2.2	27.2	65.1	3.1
financial	public	31.1	2.7	3.8	32.1	57.7	3.7
exigency	private	22.3	1.8	0.3	21.2	74.3	2.4
Laying off tenured	all	20.4	2.6	4.5	44.9	42.4	5.7
faculty because of	public	20.5	3.1	5.0	39.1	46.5	6.4
financial exigency	private	20.2	2.0	3.8	51.6	37.3	4.9
Laying off nontenured	all	23.6	6.4	16.7	42.7	29.6	4.6
faculty because of	public	25.1	4.5	9.5	42.8	38.9	4.2
financial exigency	private	21.8	8.6	25.2	42.6	18.5	5.1

PART II

We would like your assessment of how important each of the following academic issues is to your institution today, and how important it is likely to be three years from now. Please use the following rating scheme:

0—Do not know

1—Not important

2—Moderately important

3—Very important

ISSUE	INSTITUTION GROUP	IMPORTANCE NOW				IMPORTANCE IN 3 YEARS			
		0	1	2	3	0	1	2	3
Revising the institution's mission to respond to changes in internal or external circumstances	all	0.8	27.9	33.0	38.3	5.3	13.2	33.0	48.6
	public	0.8	21.0	34.3	43.9	5.3	9.2	32.0	53.6
	private	0.8	36.3	31.4	31.4	5.2	18.1	34.3	42.4
Determining, reviewing, and approving new academic programs	all	0.5	9.6	35.0	54.9	1.9	3.1	32.1	62.8
	public	0.3	7.7	33.3	58.7	1.4	1.6	28.7	68.3
	private	0.7	11.9	37.1	50.3	2.6	5.0	36.2	56.0
Reviewing the strengths and weaknesses of current academic programs	all	0.4	5.4	32.5	61.7	2.1	3.1	30.1	64.7
	public	0.3	4.4	31.3	64.0	1.9	3.2	30.3	64.4
	private	0.4	6.6	34.0	56.0	2.3	3.1	29.9	64.7
Determining programs to reduce, eliminate, or consolidate	all	1.5	14.6	30.2	53.7	3.7	6.7	28.7	60.9
	public	2.3	9.7	26.4	61.6	3.8	5.5	30.0	60.7
	private	0.4	20.6	34.9	44.0	3.6	8.2	27.0	61.3
Changing faculty appointment, promotion, and tenure policies to achieve greater flexibility	all	3.7	30.8	38.2	27.4	6.6	18.4	38.5	36.5
	public	5.4	27.1	40.3	27.3	9.0	19.0	39.3	32.8
	private	1.7	35.2	35.6	27.4	3.8	17.7	37.6	40.9

ISSUE	INSTITUTION GROUP	IMPORTANCE NOW				IMPORTANCE IN 3 YEARS			
		0	1	2	3	0	1	2	3
Establishing faculty evaluation procedures in order to improve the performance of faculty members	all	3.4	21.4	43.0	32.2	4.3	19.1	39.1	37.5
	public	5.1	18.7	45.6	30.5	5.7	17.6	42.2	34.5
	private	1.2	24.6	39.9	34.3	2.7	20.9	35.3	41.2
Establishing faculty development programs in order to provide faculty with opportunities for professional growth	all	0.6	16.8	45.0	37.6	2.0	8.6	44.6	44.9
	public	0.8	16.0	41.7	41.5	3.3	9.7	39.1	47.9
	private	0.3	17.8	49.1	32.9	0.4	7.1	51.3	41.2
Establishing faculty development programs in order to encourage faculty to retrain and shift to fields with greater student demand	all	3.2	31.7	35.1	30.0	6.1	18.7	36.6	38.6
	public	2.5	23.4	35.7	38.4	6.4	14.5	32.3	46.8
	private	4.1	41.9	34.4	19.7	5.8	23.8	41.8	28.6
Establishing compensation policies that place greater emphasis on merit than "across the board" increases	all	2.2	25.4	32.8	39.6	4.2	18.7	31.6	45.5
	public	3.3	25.8	30.9	40.0	5.3	18.6	32.0	44.0
	private	0.9	24.9	35.0	39.2	2.7	18.8	31.1	47.3
Establishing a planning and budgeting process that leads to rational allocation of resources to academic areas	all	1.1	13.3	27.5	58.1	2.8	8.9	27.3	61.0
	public	1.0	11.1	28.7	59.1	2.2	9.6	26.8	61.4
	private	1.2	15.9	26.0	56.8	3.5	8.0	28.0	60.6
Developing policies to govern the layoffs of full-time faculty for reasons of financial exigency	all	2.3	35.2	36.2	26.3	7.5	23.6	37.9	31.1
	public	1.5	28.6	35.5	33.4	7.7	18.9	41.1	32.4
	private	3.4	43.2	35.8	17.6	7.2	29.1	34.1	29.6
Changing admissions standards in order to alter the size or composition of the student body	all	8.9	51.3	28.6	11.3	12.5	38.3	35.6	13.6
	public	8.4	52.7	25.4	13.5	12.4	41.6	32.8	13.1
	private	9.5	49.6	32.4	8.5	12.6	34.4	38.8	14.2

ISSUE	INSTITUTION GROUP	IMPORTANCE NOW				IMPORTANCE IN 3 YEARS			
		0	1	2	3	0	1	2	3
Altering general education requirements to reflect shifts in thinking about students' educational needs and interests	all	4.6	28.1	43.3	23.9	8.4	22.0	43.4	26.2
	public	3.9	27.0	46.0	23.1	7.8	23.0	45.2	24.0
	private	5.5	29.5	40.1	24.9	9.1	20.8	41.2	29.0
Modifying policies on faculty workload or student-faculty ratios in order to increase productivity or lower costs	all	2.2	25.5	40.0	32.3	4.9	19.3	37.5	38.3
	public	3.3	22.4	36.2	38.1	6.6	16.0	38.3	39.1
	private	0.8	29.4	44.7	25.2	2.7	23.3	36.5	37.4
Establishing affirmative action policies, goals, and timetables in order to hire and retain more female and minority faculty members	all	3.0	35.9	38.6	22.5	5.9	29.1	39.2	25.8
	public	2.8	27.5	41.3	28.3	6.3	22.8	40.6	30.3
	private	3.2	45.8	35.3	15.6	5.4	36.7	37.4	20.5

PART III

1. What are your board's sources of information on academic matters? Rank in order all responses that apply, with one (1) designating the most important source.

	RANK ORDER OF RESPONSES				
	1	2	3	4	5
Academic administrators (e.g., vice president, povost, deans)	29.9	59.1	7.3	1.1	0.7
Board staff (e.g., board secretary)	3.3	6.4	8.0	3.8	3.5
External sources (e.g., publications)	0.7	2.9	19.9	13.8	14.3
Faculty government (e.g., faculty council, faculty senate)	1.9	5.0	35.2	19.0	4.8
Individual faculty members	1.0	1.1	14.8	24.9	16.3
President	67.8	21.7	4.1	0.3	1.7
Student government	0.7	0.7	0.6	13.6	14.3

2A. What type(s) of academic information does the board receive regularly? Check all responses that apply.

	RECEIVE	NEED BUT DO NOT RECEIVE
Admissions data (applications, acceptances, profile of applicants)	78.5	—
Descriptive data on current students (e.g., test score and grade distributions)	61.5	2.3
Descriptive data on faculty (e.g., tenure, salary, and workload distributions)	66.0	3.5
Descriptive data on the institution's environment (e.g., demographics of potential student population, job market trends for graduates)	69.9	1.2
Evaluative data on faculty (e.g., evidence of teaching success and research productivity)	32.7	—
Evaluative information on academic administrators	38.0	1.0
Information on curriculum and academic requirements	63.0	—

2B. Are you satisfied with the amount and quality of this information?

yes   82.5   no   17.5

3A. By what means does your board communicate with faculty? Rank in order all responses that apply, with one (1) designating the most common means of communication.

	RANK ORDER OF RESPONSES			
	1	2	3	4
No communication	2.4	0.6	1.0	6.5
Academic administrators describe faculty viewpoints	45.2	34.8	14.6	5.3
Contact with representatives or committees of faculty government	21.0	25.4	0.04	
Informal contact with individual faculty members	8.7	24.8	31.7	26.4
Faculty membership on the board or its committees	23.0	10.2	10.2	5.1

3B. Of these means of communication, which do you find the most informative? Rank in order all responses that apply, with one (1) designating the most informative means of communication.

	RANK ORDER OF RESPONSES			
	1	2	3	4
Academic administrators describe faculty viewpoints	53.7	28.6	12.0	5.8
Contact with representatives or committees of faculty government	26.3	24.5	18.3	7.3
Informal contact with individual faculty members	11.4	25.2	34.3	17.9
Faculty membership on the board or its committees	16.8	16.6	11.1	8.0

Case Studies

The eight case studies summarized below were developed expressly for the project on "Trustee Responsibility for Academic Affairs." Each case describes the approach or reaction of a board of trustees to key academic issues the college or university faced, and each case presents problems to clarify, alternatives to evaluate, and decisions to reach. Although disguised, these are real cases based on materials gathered by the authors during site visits. The cases are drawn from all sectors of higher education.

The case studies should be particularly useful as a means of initiating a discussion at a board retreat or at a special meeting of the Academic Affairs Committee. It is often easier for participants at a retreat or workshop to discuss first academic and organizational problems that have arisen at another, preferably comparable, institution. During the course of a case discussion, participants can speak more freely, assume new roles (e.g., a trustee can adopt a professor's perspective), gain new insights, and draw parallels between the case and local circumstances.

To facilitate the discussion, the authors have prepared for each case an analysis of the situation and the board's response as well as a set of questions to provide focus. These aids should help the discussion leader—whether an insider or an external resource person—guide the deliberations.

The cases might also be useful in faculty/staff seminars, executive education programs, or graduate school courses. Copies of the cases are available at a modest cost per case from:

Trustee Information Center
Association of Governing Boards
Suite 400
One Dupont Circle
Washington, D.C. 20036

DAWSON STATE UNIVERSITY SYSTEM

RICHARD P. CHAIT
16 pages

The Board of Trustees of the Dawson State University System has responsibility for three community colleges, two four-year colleges, and two universities. The board recently completed a revision of the Academic Policy Manual, a compendium of personnel policies and procedures, an action that caused considerable strain between the board and the several faculties.

The trustees are unusually accessible to all constituencies for informal as well as formal communication. This approach reflects the "Dawson way," an inclination toward populism.

Until recently, the board had four standing committees, including one for academic affairs; now the board operates as a committee of the whole.

HUNTVALE COLLEGE

MIRIAM M. WOOD
14 pages

Huntvale is a church-related, residential, liberal arts college which enrolls fewer than 1,000 students. An accreditation report first alerted members of the governing board to a new conception of their responsibilities, and subsequently professional consultants retained by the board concluded that the college was in precarious financial condition.

Financial instability, the trustees have since learned, is the result of Huntvale's problems in attracting and retaining students and of an imbalance between what the faculty is prepared to teach and what the students are asking to learn. Working with its consultants, the board has recently hired a new president. In the face of faculty resistance, the board plans to raise the student-faculty ratio and has begun to redefine the college's mission, although some disagreement exists within the board on this matter. If funds are allocated in accordance with the emerging pattern of new academic priorities, the faculty will be divided into winners from the professional/vocational side of the curriculum and losers from the arts and humanities side.

In a situation where the survival of the college is at stake, the board has neglected to cultivate the leadership potential of the president, and the president has backed away from academic issues, claiming to be out of his element.

PHELPS INSTITUTE OF TECHNOLOGY

BARBARA E. TAYLOR
12 pages

Phelps Institute of Technology is a large, doctorate-granting public university governed by a nine-member, state-appointed board of trustees. The board is relatively inactive in the academic sphere, delegating most decision making authority to the president, in whom the board expresses singular trust.

The Academic Affairs Committee is probably the least active board committee, and confines itself mainly to discussing and approving the administration's recommendations. Trustees define their main responsibilities as lobbying and fund raising, and their success is apparent in Phelps's comparatively generous budget.

Despite the appearance of openness and informality at board and committee meetings, actual trustee influence on the institution is exercised quite privately. This probably results from the state law requiring all board and committee meetings to be open to the public.

RENWICK UNIVERSITY

MIRIAM M. WOOD
12 pages

With an enrollment of 8,500 students, Renwick University has seven professional schools in addition to an undergraduate college and a graduate school of arts and sciences. This private university is located in a metropolitan area, and over 2,000 students are attending part time.

A standing committee of the board, the University Plans Committee, periodically oversees the development of a five-year plan, the most recent of which established "greater distinction" as the university's academic objective. Otherwise, the board has little influence on faculty and curriculum affairs and has delegated monitoring the academic programs to a Board of Overseers whose chairman is an ex officio member of the Board of Trustees.

The overseers set up visiting committees for each school and over 300 people, including experts in particular fields and alumni/ae, as well as persons whom the university would like to cultivate, are involved in academic overseeing. At least every two years a report to the board is made concerning Overseer and Visiting Committee activities; otherwise the Visiting Committees relate directly to the deans of the various schools and to members of the central administration. Trustees may serve on the Visiting Committee, but very few do.

SHERIDAN COMMUNITY COLLEGE

BARBARA E. TAYLOR
14 pages

Sheridan Community College is governed by a nine member elected board of trustees. Trustees and administrators are usually friendly and cooperative, often referring to themselves as a family. The college president and board chairman interact frequently and informally to work out potential differences of opinion among trustees and between trustees and administrators before recommendations are brought to the board.

The board does not typically involve itself in the details of academic affairs. This is a measure of the board's trust in the president, as well as the president's skill in managing both the institution and his own relationship with the board. Faculty generally support the board's and administration's academic decisions, though they also express some frustration at not being powerful enough to influence these decisions significantly.

THAYER STATE COLLEGE

BARBARA E. TAYLOR
15 pages

Thayer State College is a comprehensive public institution governed by a highly active, state-appointed board of trustees. The board's Personnel and Academic Program Committees explain that they—and the board as a whole—involve themselves in the specifics of academic affairs out of concern for Thayer's academic integrity and flexibility.

The board recently adopted a new institutional mission statement after only minimal consultation with the administration and none with the faculty. This action, which resulted in a lawsuit by the faculty against the board, strained further an already distrustful relationship between the two groups. It also reinforced a view prevalent among faculty members that the administration is too weak to influence the board.

WINTER COLLEGE

KENNETH P. MORTIMER
21 pages

Winter College is a selective private college of about 4,000 students located in the northeast. While primarily an undergraduate college, it has graduate programs in business, engineering, medicine, and the sciences.

The sixteen member Board of Trustees meets quarterly and is characterized as very active. The Board's Committee on Educational Affairs, which once focused on a question of facilities, now concentrates on educational issues. Deliberations take place in an atmosphere of deference to faculty and administrative expertise. Trustees ask three questions: Will the college be proud of the effort? Is it financially feasible? Will it support—or at least not harm—the undergraduate programs?

The analytic section of the case argues that Winter College has a broadly based consensus about its major commitments and that board/administration understandings are an important product of that consensus. Board members and many administrators are alumni/ae and/or share long-standing commitments to the college.

On purely educational affairs, the board delegates significant authority to the faculty and administration, retaining only its right of review and veto. On matters of educational policy that have substantial fiscal implications, the board solicits advice from a variety of sources but makes its own decisions.

WESTERN FLAGSHIP UNIVERSITY

KENNETH P. MORTIMER
19 pages

Western Flagship University is a large (over 30,000 students) public institution located in an urban area of a western state. It is a research-oriented institution with a wide range of colleges and professional schools.

The seven members of the Board of Trustees are appointed by the governor to five-year terms, and many are reappointed. Four ex officio board members represent the faculty, the graduate and the undergraduate students, and the alumni/ae.

At monthly board meetings, committees meet first, followed by a meeting as a Committee of the Whole. The board then convenes in formal session. An executive session may follow.

The Committee on Student Affairs reviews and makes recommendations on the budget, faculty personnel policies, educational policy, student activity fees, and student welfare. It is the conduit through which these issues flow to the full board for action. As such, the committee probes, questions and has the power to delay, change, and/or veto proposals. In practice it usually follows administrative recommendations.

The board's monthly meetings are well attended and each trustee serves on at least one committee. The board's role in academic policy is characterized as one of active interest and influence.

Trustees have regular and sustained consultation with senior administrators. Many have direct ties to faculty and administrators and are generally knowledgeable about educational matters. When a financial emergency was declared, the board and its individual members expressed in a variety of nonpublic but direct ways its concern about minimizing the effects of fiscal stringencies on academic quality.

Recommended Readings

CHAPTER II

Guidelines for an Academic Affairs Committee

The reader might find it useful to peruse the following resources for additional information on trustee roles and responsibilities, particularly in regard to academic management.

Keller (1983) provides a readable and perceptive analysis of ways in which successful academic plans are formulated. The key chapter, "Shaping Academic Strategy," cites specific institutional examples.

Nason (1982), often considered the foremost observer of trusteeship, describes 13 major responsibilities of governing boards and 14 organizational factors associated with effective boards.

Wood (1983) describes the "operating styles" of governing boards, and shows that a board's attention to managerial issues detracts from a more useful role in the development of institutional strategy.

In this easy-to-read volume, Zander (1977) analyzes the behavior of small groups and offers practical advice for making committees function more effectively.

CHAPTER III

Academic Personnel Policy and Administration

The select annotated bibliography presented here should serve as a guide for trustees who have a desire or interest to explore academic personnel policies more fully.

Academic Tenure

Chait (1980) discusses rather extensively the board's responsibility for "Setting Tenure and Personnel Policies." Chait and Ford (1982) examine the alternatives to and modifications of traditional tenure as well as the policies and procedures that contribute to an effective conventional tenure system.

For a balanced view of the policy recommendations of the American Association of University Professors (AAUP), trustees would be well advised to review the *AAUP Policy Documents and Reports* (1977), the association's policy handbook and Furniss (1978), which considered and sometimes challenged the wisdom and force of AAUP policies.

Reductions in Force

Mortimer and Tierney (1979) provide an excellent introduction to the principal issues and strategies of "Reduction, Reallocation, and Retrenchment." Mingle (1981) is an informative volume of 19 chapters on such issues as strategic choices for institutions, implications for faculty, and policy options for public and private schools.

Furniss (1976) offers a well reasoned and sharp critique of the 1976 AAUP retrenchment policy and suggests alternative concepts and language for a contingency policy.

Compensation and Reward System

Although not addressed to education, Lawler (1971) is a splendid treatment of the philosophical, psychological, and practical aspects of compensation. McKeachie (1979) emphasizes the need for incentives that extend well beyond material rewards to include "payoffs" that lead to a greater sense of fulfillment and achievement.

Faculty Evaluation

Centra (1979) is a comprehensive treatment of faculty evaluation that offers sound and practical advice on assessment of teaching, research, and service. The sections on student evaluation of teaching are especially useful. While not as extensive or detailed, SREB (1979) presents a useful and workable model for faculty evaluation.

Faculty Development

The opportunities and limitations of faculty development are well stated in Blackburn (1980) and Nelson and Siegel (1980); the latter volume concentrates on liberal arts colleges. Valuable resources, often published as newsletters or pamphlets, are available from the Center for Faculty Evaluation and Development in Higher Education at Kansas State University.

Affirmative Action

Of the many treatments of the topic, the Carnegie Council report (1975) probably provides the best overview as well as helpful excerpts from various institutional policy statements.

CHAPTER IV

Academic Programs

Curriculum Reform

The Carnegie Foundation's *Missions of the College Cur-*

riculum (1977) provides a comprehensive discussion of the elements of curriculum. It includes chapters on components of the curriculum, internal and external curriculum policy, and change. Levine (1978) provides a comprehensive perspective, both comparative and historical, of the undergraduate curriculum.

Chickering et al. (1977) provides a good discussion of the obstacles to curriculum development and gives concepts, instruments, and activities for implementing and evaluating curriculum reforms.

Gaff (1983) has written a good treatment of the special problems and prospects for general education. Part 3 is an excellent discussion of the problems in implementing successful curriculum reforms.

Program Review and Closure

Craven (1980) discusses the contextual factors—historical, institutional, state agency, and accrediting agency—that are important in program evaluation and review. The last chapter is a good source of readings about programs. Anderson and Ball (1978) and Barak (1982) are comprehensive treatments of the art and prospects of program review at the institutional and state levels.

Dougherty's (1979) article discusses ten large institutions' experiences in discontinuing programs and gives helpful suggestions. Melchiori (1982) is a comprehensive treatment of discontinuing programs, and suggests how institutions can move to more planned approaches.

CHAPTER V

Academic Budgets

Among the many published works that describe budget making and financial overseeing, the following should be particularly useful.

Financial Responsibilities of Trustees

The Association of Governing Boards of Universities and Colleges and the National Association of College and University Business Officers (1979) offer a comprehensive treatment of trustees' financial responsibilities. The volume not only explains complex financial concepts clearly, but through questions, illustrations, and examples also acquaints trustees with the elements of effective financial overseeing.

The Context of Academic Budgeting

Anthony and Herzlinger (1975) describe the management of nonprofit organizations, with attention to financial control and budgeting. The book is not always easy reading, nor is it devoted entirely to colleges and universities. Nevertheless, it offers a particularly fine research based approach to understanding the nature of nonprofit organizations, the interactions of their components, and the role of finances in organizational functioning.

In contrast with Anthony and Herzlinger, Balderston (1974) is a less technical treatment of college and university management, though it also explains budgeting in an organizational context. The book is especially concerned with the allocation of constrained resources and with effective responses to the environmental pressures that affect resource acquisition.

Mortimer and Tierney (1979) are concerned specifically with the environmental pressures that afflict institutional budgets and precipitate budget reductions, reallocations, and the retrenchment of personnel. The authors offer specific examples of institutional responses to resource shortages.

Budgeting Issues

Caruthers and Orwig (1979) is a comprehensive and readable treatment of higher education budgeting issues, approaches, responsibilities, and trends. The authors examine not only the budgeting literature but also the experiences of individual institutions. Page for page, this is probably the most informative general work available on higher education budgeting.

Micek (1980) is a collection of conference papers that address the important but often difficult task of integrating academic planning and budgeting. The papers offer practical advice on such crucial topics as program planning and review in relation to financial decision making, ties between long-range plans and annual budgets, and political considerations in the budget process.

Bibliography

Allen, R. H. and Collier, D. J. "The Source-Use Concept." *Higher Education Finance Manual.* Boulder, Colorado: National Center for Higher Education Mangement Systems, 1980.

American Association of University Professors. *AAUP Policy Documents and Reports.* Washington, D.C.: American Association of University Professors, 1977.

American Association of University Professors. "1982 Recommended Institutional Regulations on Academic Freedom and Tenure." *Academe,* vol. 69, no. 1: 15a-20a.

American Association of University Professors and Association of American Colleges. Commission on Academic Tenure. *Faculty Tenure: A Report and Recommendations.* San Francisco: Jossey-Bass, 1973.

American Association of University Professors, American Council on Education, and Association of Governing Boards of Universities and Colleges. "Statement of Government of Colleges and Universities." *AAUP Bulletin,* vol. 52, no. 4: 375-379.

Anderson, S. B. and Ball, S. *The Profession and Practice of Program Evaluation.* San Francisco: Jossey-Bass, 1978.

Anthony, R. N. and Herzlinger, R. *Management Control in Nonprofit Organizations.* Homewood, Illinois: Richard D. Irwin, Inc., 1975.

Association of Governing Boards of Universities and Colleges. *The Board's Role in Accreditation.* Washington, D.C.: Association of Governing Boards of Universities and Colleges, 1982.

Association of Governing Boards of Universities and Colleges and National Association of College and University Business Officers. *Financial Responsibilities of Governing Boards of Colleges and Universities.* Washington, D.C.: Association of Governing Boards of Universities and Colleges and National Association of College and University Business Officers, 1979.

Balderston, F. E. *Managing Today's University.* San Francisco: Jossey-Bass, 1978.

Barak, R. *Program Review in Higher Education.* Boulder, Colorado: National Center for Higher Education Management Systems, 1982.

Blackburn, R. T. "Project for Faculty Development Program Evaluation: Final Report." Unpublished paper. Ann Arbor, Michigan: Center for the Study of Higher Education, University of Michigan, 1980.

Bloomfield, S. D. and Updegrove, D. A. "Modeling for Insight, Not Numbers." *EDUCOM Bulletin,* vol. 17, no. 3: 5-9.

Carnegie Council on Policy Studies in Higher Education. *Making Affirmative Action Work in Higher Education.* San Francisco: Jossey-Bass, 1975.

Carnegie Foundation for the Advancement of Teaching. *Missions of The College Curriculum: A Contemporary Review with Suggestions.* San Francisco: Jossey-Bass, 1977.

Caruthers, J. K., and Orwig, M. *Budgeting in Higher Education.* Research Report No. 3, ERIC Clearinghouse on Higher Education. Washington, D.C.: American Association for Higher Education, 1973.

Centra, J. A. *Determining Faculty Effectiveness: Assessing Teaching, Research, and Service for Personnel Decisions and Improvement.* San Francisco: Jossey-Bass, 1979.

Chait, R. P. "Academic Management: What It Should Be." In L. W. Jones and F. A. Nowotny, (eds.) *New Directions for Higher Education: Preparing for the New Decade,* no. 28. San Francisco: Jossey-Bass, 1980.

Chait, R. P. "Setting Tenure and Personnel Policies." In R. T. Ingram and Associates, *Handbook of College and University Trusteeship: A Practical Guide for Trustees, Chief Executive Officers, and Other Leaders Responsible for Developing Effective Governing Boards.* San Francisco: Jossey-Bass, 1980.

Chait, R. P. and Ford, A. T. *Beyond Traditional Tenure: A Guide to Sound Policies and Practices.* San Francisco: Jossey-Bass, 1982.

Chickering, A. W., Halliburton, D., Berquist, W., and Lindquist, J. *Developing the College Curriculum: A Handbook for Faculty and Administrators.* Washington, D.C.: Council for the Advancement of Small Colleges, 1977.

Classification of Institutions of Higher Education. Berkeley, California: Carnegie Commission on Higher Education, 1973.

Cohen, M. D., and March, J. G. *Leadership and Ambiguity: The American College President.* New York: McGraw Hill, 1974.

Conference Board of Associated Research Councils. *An Assessment of Research-Doctorate Programs in the United States.* Washington, D.C.: National Academy Press, 1982.

Corson, J. J. "Participating in Policy Making and Management." In R. T. Ingram and Associates, *Handbook of College and University Trusteeship: A Practical Guide for Trustees, Chief Executives, and Other Leaders Responsible for Developing Effective Governing Boards.* San Francisco: Jossey-Bass, 1980.

Craven, E. C. *New Directions for Institutional Research: Academic Program Evaluation,* no. 27. San Francisco: Jossey-Bass, 1980.

Cross, K. P. *Beyond the Open Door: New Students to Higher Education.* San Francisco: Jossey-Bass, 1971.

Davis, D. K., and Dougherty, E. A. "Program Discontinuance: Its Role in Strategies of Resource Allocation and Planning for Colleges and Universities." Mimeographed. Ann Arbor, Michigan: University of Michigan, no date.

Dougherty, E. A. "What Is The Most Effective Way To Handle Program Discontinuance?" *Current Issues in Higher Education,* 1979, no. 5: 25-34.

Furniss, W. T. "The 1976 AAUP Retrenchment Policy." *Educational Record,* vol. 57 no. 3: 133-139.

Furniss, W. T. "Status of AAUP Policy." *Educational Record,* vol. 59, no. 1: 7-29.

Gaff, J. *General Education Today.* San Francisco: Jossey-Bass, 1983.

Ingram, R. T., and Associates. *Handbook of College and University Trusteeship: A Practical Guide for Trustees, Chief Executives, and Other Leaders Responsible for Developing Effective Governing Boards.* San Francisco: Jossey-Bass, 1980.

Keller, G. *Academic Strategy: The Management Revolution in American Higher Education.* Baltimore: The Johns Hopkins University Press, 1983.

Lawler, E. E., III. *Pay and Organizational Effectiveness: A Psychological View.* New York: McGraw-Hill, 1971.

Levine, A. *Handbook on Undergraduate Curriculum.* San Francisco: Jossey-Bass, 1978.

McKeachie, W. J. "What Motivates Academic Behavior?" In D. R. Lewis and W. E. Becker (eds.), *Academic Rewards in Higher Education.* Cambridge, Massachusetts: Ballinger, 1979.

Melchiori, G. S. *Planning for Program Discontinuance: From Default to Design.* Research Report No. 5, ERIC Clearinghouse on Higher Education. Washington, D.C.: American Association for Higher Education, 1982.

Micek, S. S. (ed.). *Integrating Academic Planning and Budgeting in a Rapidly Changing Environment.* Boulder, Colorado: National Center for Higher Education Management Systems, 1980.

Mingle, J. R., and Associates. *Challenges of Retrenchment: Strategies for Consolidating Programs, Cutting Costs, and Reallocating Resources.* San Francisco: Jossey-Bass, 1981.

Minter, J. W., Nelson, C. A., and Robinson, D. D. *Ratio Analysis in Higher Education.* New York: Peat, Marwick, Mitchell and Co., 1980.

Miyataki, G. K., and Byers, M. L. *Academic Unit Planning and Management.* Technical Report 75. Boulder, Colorado: National Center for Higher Education Management Systems, January 1976.

Mortimer, K. P., and Tierney, M. L. *The Three "R's" of the Eighties: Reduction, Reallocation, and Retrenchment.* Research Report No. 4, ERIC Clearinghouse on Higher Education. Washington, D.C.: American Association for Higher Education, 1979.

Nason, John W. *The Future of Trusteeship: The Role and Responsibilities of College and University Boards.* Washington, D.C.: Association of Governing Boards of Universities and Colleges, 1975.

Nason, John W. *The Nature of Trusteeship: The Role and Responsibilities of College and University Boards.* Washington, D.C.: Association of Governing Boards of Universities and Colleges, 1982.

Nason, John W. *Trustee Responsibilities.* Washington, D.C.: Association of Governing Boards of Universities and Colleges, 1980.

National Center for Education Statistics. *Digest of Education Statistics.* Washington, D.C.: U.S. Government Printing Office, 1981.

Nelsen, W. C., and Siegel, M. E. (eds.). *Effective Approaches to Faculty Development.* Washington, D.C.: Association of American Colleges, 1980.

Shirley, R. C., and Volkwein, F. M. "Establishing Academic Priorities." *Journal of Higher Education,* vol. 49, no. 5: 472-488.

Southern Regional Education Board. *Faculty Evaluation for Improved Learning.* Atlanta: Southern Regional Education Board, 1977.

Stadtman, V. A. *Academic Adaptations: Higher Education Prepares for the 1980s and 1990s.* San Francisco: Jossey-Bass, 1980.

Stonich, P. J. *Implementing Strategy: Making Strategy Happen.* Cambridge, Massachusetts: Ballinger, 1982.

Wood, M. M. "What Role for College Trustees?" *Harvard Business Review,* vol. 61, no. 3: 52-54; 58-62.

Zander, A. *Groups at Work: Unresolved Issues in the Study of Organizations.* San Francisco: Jossey-Bass, 1977.

COURT CASES

1. *AAUP v. Bloomfield College,* 332 A.2d 846 (1974); 346 A.2d 615 (1975)

2. *Johnson v. Board of Regents of the University of Wisconsin System,* 377 F. Supp. 227 (1974).

3. *Lumpert v. University of Dubuque,* 255 N.W. 2d 168 (1977).

4. *NLRB v. Yeshiva University,* 44 U.S. 672 (1980).

5. *Scheuer v. Creighton University,* 260 N.W.2d 595 (1977).

Index